READINGS IN LENINISM
No. 4

STRATEGY AND TACTICS
OF THE
PROLETARIAN REVOLUTION

First Published in the United States, 1936

Republished by Red Star Publishers, 2014
www.RedStarPublishers.org

NOTE

This volume is one of a series of "Readings in Leninism." Each book consists of a collection of articles and extracts – taken almost exclusively from the works of Marx, Engels, Lenin and Stalin – dealing with a basic question of Leninist theory.

The key passages included in these volumes are not designed to serve as a substitute for reading the fundamental works of Marxism-Leninism in their entirety. The purpose of the series is to assemble, within the covers of a single book, pertinent excerpts dealing with a specific problem of primary importance, such as the theory of the proletarian revolution, the dictatorship of the proletariat, strategy and tactics of the proletarian revolution, the national and agrarian questions, etc.

Systematically compiled and arranged by V. Bystryansky and M. Mishin, this material should be extremely helpful as a guide to individual or group study of the fundamental principles of Leninism.

The present volume analyzes the nature of Bolshevik strategy and tactics and contrasts it with the program and measures of reformist leadership.

CONTENTS

I. FORMULATION OF THE QUESTION OF STRATEGY AND TACTICS IN LENINISM

1. Bolshevik Strategy and Tactics as a Science of Leadership of the Class Struggle of the Proletariat

The period of the domination of the Second International was mainly the period of the formation and instruction of the proletarian armies in an environment of more or less peaceful development. This was the period when parliamentarism was the outstanding form of class struggle. Questions of great class conflicts, of preparing the proletariat for revolutionary combats, of the ways and means leading to the conquest of the dictatorship of the proletariat, did not seem to be on the order of the day at that time. The task reduced itself to utilizing all paths of legal development for the formation and instruction of the armies of proletarians; for the utilization of parliamentarism in conformity with the conditions under which the proletariat was (and as it seemed then, was destined to remain) in the opposition. It need hardly be pointed out that during such a period and with such a conception of the tasks of the proletariat, there could be neither complete strategy nor any elaborated tactics. There were fragmentary and detached ideas about tactics and strategy, but no tactics or strategy as such.

The mortal sin of the Second International was not that it adopted the tactic of utilizing the parliamentary forms of struggle, but that it overestimated the importance of these forms, that it considered them to be virtually the only forms; and when the period of open revolutionary combats arrived and the question of extra-parliamentary forms of struggle came to the fore, the parties of the Second International turned their backs on these new tasks and refused to shoulder them.

Only in the subsequent period, the period of direct action by the proletariat, in the period of proletarian revolution, when the question of the overthrow of the bourgeoisie became a question of immediate practice, when the question of the reserves of the proletariat (strategy) became one of the most burning questions, when all forms of struggle and of organization, parliamentary and extra-parliamentary (tactics), assumed definite shape – only in this period could a complete strategy and detailed tactics for the struggle of the proletariat be elaborated. It was precisely in that period that Lenin dragged into the light of day the brilliant ideas of Marx and

5

Engels on tactics and strategy, that had been immured by the opportunists of the Second International. But Lenin did not rest content with restoring certain tactical theses of Marx and Engels. He developed them further and supplemented them with new ideas and new theses, correlating them all in a system of rules and guiding principles for the leadership of the class struggle of the proletariat. Lenin's pamphlets, such as *What Is To Be Done?; Two Tactics; Imperialism; The State and Revolution; The Proletarian Revolution and Renegade Kautsky; "Left-Wing" Communism, etc.*, will doubtless be treasured as priceless contributions to the general store of Marxism and to its revolutionary arsenal. The strategy and tactics of Leninism constitute the science of leadership of the revolutionary struggle of the proletariat.

Joseph Stalin, *Leninism*, Vol. I, pp. 72-73.

2. First Principles of Strategy and Tactics of the Proletariat and Examples from Marx and Engels

Having discovered as early as 1844-45[*] that one of the chief defects of the earlier materialism was its failure to understand the conditions or recognize the importance of practical revolutionary activity, Marx, during all his life, along with his theoretical work, gave unremitting attention to the tactical problems of the class struggle of the proletariat. An immense amount of material bearing upon this is contained in *all* the works of Marx and particularly in the four volumes of his correspondence with Engels (*Briefwechsel*), published in 1913. This material is still far from having been collected, systematized, studied, and elaborated. This is why we shall have to confine ourselves to the most general and brief remarks, emphasizing the point that Marx justly considered materialism without *this* side to be incomplete, one-sided, and devoid of vitality. The fundamental task of proletarian tactics was defined by Marx in strict conformity with the general principles of his materialist-dialectical outlook. Nothing but an objective account of the totality of all the mutual relationships of all the classes of a given society without exception, and consequently an account of the objective stage of development of this society as well as an

---

[*] Lenin refers here to Marx's and Engels' works: *The Holy Family, German Ideology* and Marx's *Theses on Feuerbach. – Ed.*

account of the mutual relationship between it and other societies, can serve as the basis for the correct tactics of the advanced class. All classes and all countries are at the same time looked upon not statically, but dynamically; *i.e.,* not as motionless, but as in motion (the laws of their motion being determined by the economic conditions of existence of each class). The motion, in its turn, is looked upon not only from the point of view of the past, but also from the point of view of the future; and, moreover, not only in accordance with the vulgar conception of the "evolutionists," who see only slow changes – but dialectically: "In developments of such magnitude, twenty years are more than a day – so later on days may come in which twenty years are embodied," wrote Marx to Engels (*Briefwechsel,* Vol. III, p. 127).

At each stage of development, at each moment, proletarian tactics must take account of these objectively unavoidable dialectics of human history, utilizing, on the one hand, the periods of political stagnation, or periods when things are moving at a snail's pace along the road of so-called "peaceful" development, to increase the class consciousness, strength, and fighting capacity of the advanced class; on the other hand, conducting this work in the direction of the "final aim" of the movement of this class, cultivating in it the faculty for practically carrying out great tasks in great days in which "twenty years are embodied." Two of Marx's arguments are of especial importance in this connection: one of these is in *The Poverty of Philosophy,* and relates to the industrial struggle and to the industrial organizations of the proletariat; the other is in *The Communist Manifesto,* and relates to the proletariat's political tasks. The former runs as follows:

> Large-scale industry concentrates in one place a crowd of people unknown to one another. Competition divides their interests. But the maintenance of wages, this common interest which they have against their boss, unites them in a common thought of resistance – *combination...* combinations, at first isolated, constitute themselves into groups, as the capitalists in their turn unite in the idea of repression, and in face of always-united capital, the maintenance of the association becomes more necessary to them than that of wages.... In this struggle – a veritable civil war – are united and developed all the elements necessary for a coming battle. Once it has reached this point, association takes on a

7

political character.[*]

Here we have the program and the tactics of the economic struggle and the trade union movement for several decades to come, for the whole long period in which the workers are preparing for "a future battle." We must place side by side with this a number of references by Marx and Engels to the example of the British labor movement; how, in consequence of industrial "prosperity," attempts are made "to buy the workers" (*Briefwechsel*, Vol. I, p. 136), to distract them from the struggle; how, generally speaking, this prosperity "demoralizes the workers" (Vol. II, p. 218); how the British proletariat is becoming "bourgeoisified"; how "the ultimate aim of this most bourgeois of all nations seems to be to establish a bourgeois aristocracy and a bourgeois proletariat side by side with the bourgeoisie" (Vol. II, p. 290); how the "revolutionary energy" of the British proletariat oozes away (Vol. III, p. 124); how it will be necessary to wait for a considerable time before the British workers can rid themselves of their apparent bourgeois corruption." (Vol. III, p. 127); how the British movement "lacks the mettle of the Chartists" (1866: Vol. III, p. 305); how the British workers' leaders are developing into something between "a radical bourgeois and a worker" (Vol. IV, p. 209, on Holyoake); how, owing to British monopoly, and as long as that monopoly lasts, "the British workingman will not budge" (Vol. IV, p. 433). The tactics of the economic struggle, in connection with the general course (and *the outcome*) of the labor movement, are here considered from a remarkably broad, many-sided, dialectical, and genuinely revolutionary outlook.

On the tactics of the political struggle, the *Communist Manifesto* advanced this fundamental Marxian thesis:

> The Communists fight for the attainment of the immediate aims, for the enforcement of the momentary interests of the working class; but in the movement of the present, they also represent and take care of the future of that movement.[†]

---

[*] Karl Marx, *The Poverty of Philosophy,* p. 145, London and New York, 1936. – *Ed.*

[†] *Communist Manifesto,* p. 43, London and New York, 1933. – *Ed.*

That was why, in 1848, Marx supported the Polish party of the "agrarian revolution" – "the party which initiated the Cracow insurrection in the year 1846." In Germany during 1848 and 1849 he supported the radical revolutionary democracy, and subsequently never retracted what he had then said about tactics. He looked upon the German bourgeoisie as "inclined from the very beginning to betray the people" (only an alliance with the peasantry would have enabled the bourgeoisie completely to fulfill its tasks) "and to compromise with the crowned representatives of the old order of society." Here is Marx's summary account of the class position of the German bourgeoisie at the time of the bourgeois-democratic revolution – an analysis which, among other things, is an example of that materialism, which considers society in motion, and not only that part of the motion which is directed *backwards!*

Lacking faith in themselves, lacking faith in the people; grumbling at those above, and trembling in face of those below... dreading a world-wide storm... nowhere with energy, everywhere with plagiarism... without initiative... – a miserable old man, doomed to guide in his own senile interests the first youthful impulses of a young and vigorous people.... (*Neue Rheinische Zeitung,* 1848; see *Literarischer Nachlass,* Vol. III, p. 213.)

About twenty years afterwards, writing to Engels (*Briefwechsel,* Vol. III, p. 224), Marx said that the cause of the failure of the Revolution of 1848 was that the bourgeoisie had preferred peace with slavery to the mere *prospect* of having to fight for freedom. When the revolutionary period of 1848-49 was over, Marx was strongly opposed to any playing at revolution (Schapper and Willich, and the fight with them), insisting on the need for knowing how to work under the new conditions, when quasi-"peacefully" new revolutions were in the making. The spirit in which Marx wanted the work to be carried on is plainly shown by his estimate of the situation in Germany during the period of blackest reaction in 1856: "The whole thing in Germany will depend on the possibility of backing the proletarian revolution by some second edition of the Peasant War." (*Briefwechsel,* Vol. II, p. 108).

While the bourgeois-democratic revolution in Germany was in progress, Marx directed his whole attention, in the matter of tactics of the socialist proletariat, to developing the democratic energy of the peasantry. He held that Lassalle's action was "objectively... a betrayal of the whole workers' movement to the Prussians" (*Briefwechsel,* Vol. III, p. 210), among other things, because he "favored the *Junkers* and Prussian Nationalism." On February 5, 1865, exchanging views with Marx regarding a forthcoming joint declaration of theirs in the press, Engels wrote (*Briefwechsel,* Vol. III, p. 217):

> ...In a predominantly agricultural country... it is dastardly to make an exclusive attack on the bourgeoisie in the name of the industrial proletariat, but never to devote a word to the patriarchal exploitation of the rural proletariat under the lash of the great feudal aristocracy....

During the period from 1864 to 1870, when the epoch of the bourgeois-democratic revolution in Germany, that epoch of the fight of the exploiting classes of Prussia and Austria for completing the revolution *from above,* in one way or another, was coming to an end, Marx not only condemned Lassalle for coquetting with Bismarck, but also corrected Wilhelm Liebknecht, who had lapsed into "Austrophilism" and defended particularism. Marx insisted upon revolutionary tactics that would fight against both Bismarck and "Austrophilism" with equal ruthlessness, tactics that would not only suit the "conqueror," the Prussian *Junker,* but would forthwith renew the struggle with him *upon the very basis* created by the Prussian military successes (*Briefwechsel,* Vol. III, pp. 134, 136, 147, 179, 204, 210, 215, 418, 437, 440, 441). In the famous Address of the International Workingmen's Association, dated September 9, 1870, Marx warned the French proletariat against an untimely uprising; but when, in 1871, the uprising actually took place, Marx hailed with the utmost enthusiasm the revolutionary initiative of the masses, who were "storming heaven."[*] In this situation, as in so many others, the defeat of a revolutionary onslaught was, from the Marxian standpoint of dialectical materialism, from the point of view of the general course and *the outcome* of the proletarian struggle, a lesser evil than would have been a retreat from a position hitherto occupied, a surrender without battle, as such a surrender would have demoralized the proletariat and undermined its

---

[*] Karl Marx: *Letters to Dr. Kugelmann,* London and New York, 1934, p. 123.

readiness for struggle. Fully recognizing the importance of using legal means of struggle during periods of political stagnation, and when bourgeois legality prevails, Marx, in 1877 and 1878, when the Exceptional Law against the Socialists had been passed in Germany, strongly condemned the "revolutionary phrase-making" of Most; but he attacked no less, and perhaps even more sharply, the opportunism that, for a time, prevailed in the official Social-Democratic Party, which, on the spur of the moment, failed to manifest resolution, firmness, revolutionary spirit, a readiness to resort to illegal struggle in reply to the Exceptional Law. (*Briefwechsel,* Vol. IV, pp. 397, 404, 418, 422, and 424; also letters to Sorge.)

V. I. Lenin, *Marx-Engels-Marxism,* pp. 29-33.

3. Leadership in a Situation and Consideration for Its Peculiarities – the Main Characteristic of Leninist Strategy and Tactics

...while the working class movement is everywhere passing through what is practically a similar preparatory school for victory over the bourgeoisie, it is in each country achieving this development in *its own way.* The big, advanced capitalist countries are marching along this road *much more rapidly* than did Bolshevism, which history granted a period of fifteen years to prepare itself for victory as an organized political trend. The Third International has already scored a decisive victory in the short space of one year; it has defeated the yellow, social-chauvinist Second International, which only a few months ago was incomparably stronger than the Third International, and which seemed to be firm and strong, enjoying the all-round support – direct and indirect, material (ministerial posts, passports, the press) and ideological – of the world bourgeoisie.

The main thing now is that the Communists of every country should quite consciously take into account the fundamental tasks of the struggle against opportunism and "Left" doctrinarism as well as the concrete *peculiar features* which this struggle assumes and inevitably must assume in each separate country in accordance with the peculiar features of its economics, politics, culture, national composition (Ireland, etc.), its colonies, religious divisions, etc. Everywhere we observe widening and growing dissatisfaction with the Second International because of its opportunism, its inability or incapability, to create a really centralized, really leading center which would be capable of guiding the international tactics of the revolutionary proletariat in its struggle for the world Soviet republic. We must clearly realize that such a leading center cannot in any circumstances be built up on stereotyped, mechanically equalized, identical tactical rules of the struggle. As long as national and state differences exist among peoples and countries – and these differences will continue to exist for a very long time, even after the dictatorship of the proletariat has been established on a world scale – the unity of international tactics of the communist working class movement of all countries demands, not the elimination of variety, not the abolition of national differences (this is a foolish dream at the present moment), but such an application of the *fundamental* principles of Communism (Soviet power and the dictatorship of the proletariat) as will *correctly modify* these principles in *certain particulars,* will properly adapt, apply them to the national and national-state differences. To investigate, study, seek out, divine, grasp that which is specifically national in the *concrete manner* in which each country *approaches* the fulfillment of the *single* international task, the victory over opportunism and "Left" doctrinarism in the working class movement, the overthrow of the bourgeoisie, the establishment of a Soviet republic and a proletarian dictatorship – this is the main task of the historical period through which all the advanced (and not only the advanced) countries are now passing. The main thing – not everything, by a long way – but the main thing has already been achieved in that the vanguard of the working class has been won over, in that it has gone over to the side of the Soviet power against parliamentarism, to the side of the dictatorship of the proletariat against bourgeois democracy. Now all efforts, all attention, must be concentrated on the *next* step – which means, and from a certain standpoint really is, less fundamental, but which in fact is much closer to the practical carrying out of the task – namely, on seeking out the forms of *transition or approach* to the proletarian revolution.

...History generally, and the history of revolutions in particular, is always richer in content, more varied, more many-sided, more lively and "subtle" than the best parties and the most class conscious vanguards of the most advanced class imagine. This is understandable, because the best vanguards express the class consciousness, the will, the passion, the phantasy of tens of thousands, while the revolution is made, at the moment of its climax and the exertion of all human capabilities, by the class consciousness, the will, the passion, and the phantasy of tens of millions who are urged on by the very acutest class struggle. From this follow two very important practical conclusions: first, that the revolutionary class, in order to fulfill its task, must be able to master *all* forms or sides of social activity without exception (and complete after the capture of political power, sometimes at great risk and amidst very great dangers, what it did not complete before the capture of power); second, that the revolutionary class must be ready to pass from one form to another in the quickest and most unexpected manner.

V. I. Lenin, *"Left-Wing" Communism: An Infantile Disorder,* pp. 71-72; 75.

4. International Significance of Bolshevik Strategy and Tactics

The Bolsheviks' tactics were correct; they were the *only* internationalist tactics, because they were based, not on the cowardly fear of a world revolution, not on a philistine "disbelief" in it, not on the narrow nationalist desire to protect "one's own" fatherland (the fatherland of one's bourgeoisie), and not "care a hang" for all the rest; they were based on a correct (and universally admitted, before the war and before the renegacy of the social-chauvinists and social-pacifists) *estimation* of the revolutionary situation in Europe. These tactics were the only internationalist tactics, because they did the utmost possible in one country for the development, support and stirring up of *the revolution in all countries.* The correctness of these tactics has been confirmed by the enormous success that has been achieved, because Bolshevism (owing, not to the merits of the Russian Bolsheviks, but to the most profound sympathy the *masses* everywhere displayed for tactics that are revolutionary in practice) has become world-Bolshevism, it has produced an idea, a theory, a program, and tactics, which differ concretely and in practice from those of social-chauvinism and social-pacifism. Bolshevism has vanquished the old, decayed International of the Scheidemanns and Kautskys, the Renaudels and Longuets, the Hendersons and the MacDonalds, who, henceforth, will be treading on each other's heels, dreaming about "unity" and trying to revive a corpse. Bolshevism *created* the ideological and tactical foundations of a Third International, a really proletarian and Communist International, which will take into consideration both the gains of the peaceful epoch and the experience of the *epoch of revolution, which has now begun.*

Bolshevism has popularized throughout the world the idea of the "dictatorship of the proletariat," has translated these words from the Latin, first into Russian, and then into *all* the languages of the world, and has shown by the living example of the *Soviet government* that the workers and poorest peasantry, *even* of a backward country, even with the least experience, education and habits of organization, *have been able* for a whole year, amidst gigantic difficulties and amidst the struggle against the exploiters (who were supported by the bourgeoisie of the *whole* world) to maintain the power of the toilers, to create a democracy that is immeasurably higher and broader than all previous democracies of the world, and to *begin,* with the aid of the creative ability of tens of millions of workers and peasants, the practical realization of socialism.

Bolshevism has helped in a practical way to develop the proletarian revolution in Europe and America more powerfully than any party in any other country has ever succeeded in doing. While the workers of the whole world are realizing more and more clearly every day that the tactics of the Scheidemanns and the Kautskys have not freed them from the imperialist war and from wage-slavery under the imperialist bourgeoisie, and that these tactics cannot serve as a model for any country, the masses of the proletarians of all countries are realizing more and more clearly every day that Bolshevism has indicated the right road of escape from the horrors of war and imperialism, that Bolshevism *can serve as a model of tactics for all.*

Not only the European, but the world proletarian revolution is maturing before the eyes of all, and it has been assisted, has been accelerated, has been supported, by the victory of the proletariat in Russia, Is all this enough for the complete victory of socialism? Certainly not. One country cannot do more. But thanks to the Soviet government, this one country has nevertheless done so much that even if the Russian Soviet government is crushed by world imperialism tomorrow, as a result of an agreement between German and Anglo-French imperialism, for example – even in this worst possible case, Bolshevik tactics will still have brought enormous benefit to Socialism, and will have assisted the growth of the invincible world revolution.

V. I. Lenin, *The Proletarian Revolution and Renegade Kautsky,* pp. 71-73.

5. Dependence of Strategy on the Party Program

A. Two Aspects of the Working Class Movement

Political strategy, like tactics, is concerned with the working class movement. But the working class movement itself consists of two elements: the objective, or spontaneous element and the subjective, or conscious element. The objective, or spontaneous element is made up of the group of processes that take place irrespective of the consciousness and regulating will of the proletariat. The economic development of the country, the development of capitalism, the disintegration of the old government, the spontaneous movements of the proletariat and the classes surrounding it, the collision of classes, and so forth – all these are phenomena, the development of which proceeds irrespective of the will of the proletariat. This is the objective aspect of the movement. Strategy is not concerned with these processes, because, it can neither stop them nor modify them; all that it can do is to reckon with them and to base itself on them. This is a field to be dealt with by the theory of Marxism and the program of Marxism.

But the movement has also a subjective, a conscious side. The subjective side of the movement consists in the reflection in the minds of the workers of the spontaneous processes of the movement; it is the conscious and deliberate movement of the proletariat towards a definite goal. This aspect of the movement interests us because, as distinct from the objective aspect of the movement, it is entirely subject to the directing influence of strategy and tactics. While strategy is unable to produce any change in the operation of the objective processes of the movement, here, on the other hand, in the subjective sphere, in relation to the conscious aspect of the movement, the field of application of strategy is broad and varied because strategy can accelerate or retard the movement, direct it along the shortest path or divert it into a more difficult and painful path, depending on the perfections or shortcomings of strategy itself.

Accelerating or retarding the movement, facilitating or hindering it, such is the field and the limits within which political strategy and tactics can be applied.

B. The Theory and Program of Marxism

Strategy is not concerned with the actual study of the objective processes of the movement. Nevertheless, it must know them and take due account of them if gross and fatal errors are not to be committed in the leadership of the movement. It is the theory of Marxism primarily and also the program of Marxism that are concerned with the study of the objective processes of the movement. Strategy, therefore, must base itself entirely on the data provided by the theory and program of Marxism.

From a study of the objective processes of capitalism in their development and decline, the theory of Marxism arrives at the conclusion that the fall of the bourgeoisie and the seizure of power by the proletariat, and the replacement of capitalism by socialism, are inevitable. Proletarian strategy may be considered truly Marxist only when it makes this fundamental conclusion of the theory of Marxism the basis of its operations.

Basing itself on the data of theory, the program of Marxism determines the aims of the proletarian movement which are scientifically formulated in the clauses of the program. The program may be designed to cover either the whole period of capitalist development to the overthrow of capitalism and the organization of socialist production, or only one specific phase in the development of capitalism, for instance, the abolition of the survivals of the feudal-absolutist system and the creation of conditions for the free development of capitalism. Accordingly, the program may consist of two parts; a maximum and a minimum. It is obvious that a strategy designed for the minimum part of the program is bound to differ from a strategy designed for the maximum part of the program. Moreover, strategy can be considered a truly Marxist strategy only when it is guided in its operations by the aims of the movement as formulated in the program of Marxism.

Joseph Stalin, "Strategy and Tactics of the Russian Communists," *Pravda,* 1923, No. 56.

II. BOLSHEVIK STRATEGY AND TACTICS

1. Strategy

A. Strategy in the Various Stages of the Revolution

Strategy is the determination of the direction of the main blow of the proletariat at a given stage of the revolution; the elaboration of a corresponding plan of disposition of the revolutionary forces (the main and secondary reserves); the struggle to carry out this plan during the whole period of the given stage of the revolution.

Our revolution had already passed through two stages and, after the October Revolution, entered upon a third stage. Our strategy was changed accordingly.

First stage, 1903 to February 1917. Aim: to overthrow tsarism and completely liquidate the survivals of medievalism. The main force of the revolution: the proletariat. Immediate reserve: the peasantry. Direction of the main blow: the isolation of the liberal-monarchist bourgeoisie which was striving to win over the peasantry and liquidate the revolution by *compromising* with tsarism. Plan for the disposition of forces: alliance of the working class with the peasantry. "The proletariat must carry out to the end the democratic revolution, and in this unite to itself the masses of the peasantry in order to crush by force the resistance of the autocracy and to paralyze the instability of the bourgeoisie." (V. I. Lenin, *Collected Works,* Russian edition, Vol. III, p. 93.)

Second stage, March 1917, to October 1917. Aim: to overthrow imperialism in Russia and to withdraw from the imperialist war. The main force of the revolution: the proletariat. Immediate reserve: the poorest peasantry. Probable reserve: the proletariat of neighboring countries. Favorable circumstances: the protracted war and the crisis of imperialism. Direction of the main blow: isolation of the petty-bourgeois democrats (Mensheviks and Socialist-Revolutionaries) who were striving to win over the toiling peasantry and put an end to the revolution by *compromising* with imperialism. Plan for the disposition of the forces: alliance of the proletariat with the poorest peasantry. "The proletariat must accomplish the socialist revolution and in this unite to itself the mass of the semi-proletarian elements of the population in order to crush by force the resistance of the bourgeoisie and to paralyse the instability of the peasantry and petty bourgeoisie." (*Ibid.*)

Third stage, commenced after the October Revolution. Aim:

consolidation of the dictatorship of the proletariat in one country, using it as a stronghold for the overthrow of imperialism in all countries. The revolution goes beyond the confines of one country and the period of world revolution commences. The main forces of the revolution: the dictatorship of the proletariat in one country and the revolutionary movement of the proletariat in all countries. Main reserves: the semi-proletarian and small peasant masses in the advanced countries and the liberation movement in the colonies and dependent countries. Direction of the main blow: the isolation of the petty-bourgeois democrats and the isolation of the parties of the Second International which constitute the main support of the policy of *compromise* with imperialism. Plan for the disposition of forces: alliance of the proletarian revolution with the liberation movement of the colonies and the dependent countries.

Strategy deals with the main forces of the revolution and their reserves. It changes with the transition of the revolution from one stage to another, but remains essentially unchanged throughout the entire duration of a given stage.

Joseph Stalin, *Leninism,* Vol. I, pp. 74-75.

B. Principal Features of Political Strategy

The most important task of strategy is to determine the main direction to be taken by the movement of the working class, the direction along which the proletariat can most advantageously deliver its main blow against its enemy in order to achieve the aims outlined in the program. A strategic plan is a plan of organization of the decisive blow in a direction in which the maximum results are most likely to be obtained.

The principal features of political strategy might easily be described by referring to military strategy for analogy: for instance, the fight with Denikin during the period of the Civil War. Everybody remembers the end of 1919, when Denikin was quartered near Tula. An interesting dispute arose at that time among military men as to where the decisive attack on the armies of Denikin should be delivered. Certain military men recommended that the line Tsaritsyn-Novorosiisk should be chosen for the decisive attack. Others, on the contrary, recommended that the decisive attack should be made along the line Voronezh-Rostov, in order, when this line had been passed and the armies of Denikin broken into two, to crush each section separately. The first plan undoubtedly had its advantages, which consisted in the fact that it calculated on the capture of Novorosiisk, which would cut off the retreat of Denikin's armies. But it was, on the one hand, disadvantageous, for it proposed that our advance should be conducted in regions (the Don) hostile to the Soviet government, which would involve considerable sacrifices; and on the other hand, it was dangerous, for it opened the way to Moscow, via Tula and Serpukhov, for the armies of Denikin. The second plan of decisive attack was the only correct plan, for, on the one hand, it proposed that the advance of our main body should be made in regions (Voronezh *gubernia* – Donets basin) sympathetic to the Soviet government, and would therefore not entail any considerable sacrifices; while, on the other hand, it would paralyze the action of the main body of Denikin's troops, which were moving on Moscow. The majority of military men declared in favor of the second plan, and this determined the fate of the whole war against Denikin.

In other words, to define the direction of the main attack is to predetermine the nature of operations during the whole war period, *i.e.,* to predetermine nine-tenths of the issue of the war. That is the task of strategy.

This also applies to political strategy. The first serious collision between the political leaders of the Russian proletariat on the question of the main direction of the proletarian movement, took place at the beginning of the twentieth century, during the Russo-Japanese war. As we know, at that time, one section of our Party (the Mensheviks) held the view that the main direction of the movement of the proletariat in its struggle against tsarism should follow along the lines of forming a *bloc* between the proletariat and the liberal bourgeoisie; the peasantry, as an important revolutionary factor, was omitted, or almost entirely omitted from the plan, while an allowance was made for the liberal bourgeoisie exercising the leadership in the general revolutionary movement. On the other hand, another section of the Party (the Bolsheviks), maintained that the main attack should assume the form of a *bloc* between the proletariat and the peasantry, that the leadership of the general revolutionary movement should be left to the proletariat, and that the liberal bourgeoisie should be neutralized.

If, by analogy with the war against Denikin, we depict our whole revolutionary movement, from the beginning of this century down to the February 1917 Revolution, as a war waged by the workers and peasants against tsarism and the landlords, it will be clear that the fate of tsarism and of the landlords to a large extent depended upon which of the two strategical plans (the Menshevik or the Bolshevik) would be adopted and what would be the main direction given to the revolutionary movement.

Just as during the war with Denikin military strategy, by indicating the main direction of the attack, determined nine-tenths of the character of all subsequent operations, including the liquidation of Denikin's armies, so here, in the sphere of the revolutionary struggle against tsarism, our political strategy, by deciding that the main direction of the revolutionary movement should follow the Bolshevik plan, determined the character of the activities of our Party during the whole period of the open struggle against tsarism, from the time of the Russo-Japanese war down to the February 1917 Revolution.

The task of political strategy primarily is, on the basis of the data provided by the theory and program of Marxism and by the experience of the revolutionary struggle of the workers of all countries, to determine the main direction of the proletarian movement of a given country in a given historical period.

Joseph Stalin, "Strategy and Tactics of the Russian Communists," *Pravda,* 1923, No. 56.

2. Tactics – a Doctrine of the Forms of Working Class Struggles

A. Tactics in Connection with the Ebb and Flow of the Revolution

Tactics are the determination of the line of conduct of the proletariat for the comparatively short period of the ebb or flow of the movement, of the rise or decline of the revolution, the struggle to carry out this line by replacing old forms of struggle and of organization by new ones, old slogans by new ones, by combining these forms, etc. While the aim of strategy is to win the war, let us say against tsarism or against the bourgeoisie, to carry the struggle against tsarism or against the bourgeoisie to its end, tactics concern themselves with less important aims, as they strive, not to win the war as a whole, but rather to win a particular engagement, or a particular battle; to carry through successfully a particular campaign or action corresponding to the concrete circumstances of the rise or decline of the revolution. Tactics are a part of strategy, subordinate and subservient to it.

Tactics change according to ebb and flow. While during the first stage of the revolution (1903 to February 1917), the strategic plan remained unchanged, tactics changed several times during that period. From 1903 to 1905 the Party pursued offensive tactics because the tide of the revolution was flowing, the movement rose and tactics had to be based on this fact.

Accordingly, the forms of struggle were revolutionary, in compliance with the requirements of the flowing tide of the revolution. Local political strikes, political demonstrations, the general political strike, the boycott of the Duma, insurrection, revolutionary fighting slogans – such were the successive changes which the struggle underwent during that period. These changes in the forms of struggle were accompanied by corresponding changes in the forms of organization. Factory and shop committees, revolutionary peasant committees, strike committees, soviets of workers' deputies, a workers' party operating more or less openly – such were the forms of organization during that period.

In the period from 1907 to 1912 the Party was compelled to resort to tactics of retreat, as we then experienced a decline in the revolutionary movement, the tide of the revolution was at an ebb, and tactics necessarily had to take this fact into consideration. The forms of struggle as well as the forms of organization were correspondingly changed: in place of the boycott of the Duma, there was participation in the Duma; in place of open, direct revolutionary action outside of the Duma, there were parliamentary speeches and work in the Duma; in place of general political strikes, there were partial economic strikes, or simply a lull in activities. Of course, the Party had to go underground during that period, while cultural, educational, cooperative, insurance and other organizations permitted by the law took the place of revolutionary mass organizations.

The same must be said of the second and third stages of the revolution during which tactics changed dozens of times whereas the strategic plans remained unchanged.

Tactics deal with the forms of struggle and the forms of organization of the proletariat, with their changes and correlations. Tactics may have to be changed several times in the period of a given stage of the revolution according to the flow and ebb, the rise and fall of the revolution.

Joseph Stalin, *Leninism,* Vol. I, pp. 75-76.

B. Tactics, a Subordinate Part of Strategy

Tactics constitute a part of strategy subordinated to it and serving it. Tactics are concerned not with war in general, but with its individual episodes, battles, and engagements. While the aim of strategy is to win the war, or, let us say, to bring the struggle against tsarism to a conclusion, the aim of tactics, on the contrary, is to win engagements and battles, and successfully to conduct campaigns and operation that are more or less suited to the concrete situation of the struggle at any given moment.

The most important task of tactics is to determine the ways and means, the forms and methods of fighting which best correspond to the concrete situation of the moment and are more certain to prepare the way for the strategical success. Consequently, the operation and results of tactics must be regarded not in isolation, not from the point of view of their immediate effect, but from the point of view of the aims and the possibilities of strategy.

There are times when tactical successes facilitate the accomplishment of strategical aims. Such was the case for instance, on the Denikin front at the end of 1919, at the time of the release of Orel and Voronezh by our troops, when the successes achieved by our cavalry at Voronezh and by our infantry at Orel created a situation favorable for the attack upon Rostov. Such was the case in August, 1917, in Russia, when the Petrograd and Moscow Soviets came over to the Bolsheviks and thereby created a new political situation which subsequently facilitated the attack launched by our Party in October.

But there are also times when tactical successes, brilliant though they may be from the point of view of their immediate success, do not correspond with the strategical possibilities, create an "unexpected" situation, which may be fatal to the whole campaign. Such was the case with Denikin at the end of 1919 when, carried away by his easy success, the rapid and effective advance on Moscow, he spread out his front from the Volga to the Dnieper and thereby brought about the defeat of his armies. Such was the case in 1920, during the war with the Poles, when we, underestimating the strength of the national factor in Poland were carried away by the easy success of an effective advance, took upon ourselves the task of breaking into Europe via Warsaw that was beyond our strength, causing the vast majority of the Polish population to rally against the Soviet army, and thereby creating a situation which nullified the successes gained by the Soviet armies at Minsk and Zhitomir and undermined the prestige of the Soviet government in the West.

Lastly, there are times when tactical successes must be ignored and when tactical disadvantages and losses must be deliberately incurred in order to insure strategical advantages in the future. This often happens in time of war, when one side, desiring to save its cadres and to remove them from the onslaught of superior forces of the enemy, undertakes a systematic retreat and surrenders whole cities and regions without a fight in order to gain time and to gather its forces for new decisive battles in the future. Such was the case in Russia in 1918, during the German advance, when our Party was forced to consent to the Peace of Brest-Litovsk, which entailed considerable disadvantages from the point of view of the immediate political effect at the moment, in order to preserve the alliance with the peasants, who were thirsting for peace, and in order to secure a respite, create a new army and thereby insure strategical advantages in the future.

In other words, tactics must not be guided by the transitory interests of the moment, they must not be guided by motives of immediate political effect, still less must they leave firm soil and build castles in the air. Tactics must be adapted to the aims and possibilities of strategy.

The duty of tactics is primarily as follows: while guided by the indications of strategy, and drawing on the experience of the revolutionary struggle of the workers of all countries, it must determine the forms and methods of fighting that are most closely in accord with the concrete situation of the struggle at the given moment.

Joseph Stalin, "Strategy and Tactics of the Russian Communists," *Pravda,* 1923, No. 56.

C. Tactics and the Choice of the Forms of Struggle

...What are the principal demands every Marxist must make when examining the question of the forms of struggle? In the first place Marxism is distinguished from all primitive forms of socialism by the fact that it does not tie the movement to any particular form of struggle. It recognizes the most varied forms of struggle. Furthermore, it does not "invent" them, but merely generalizes, organizes and makes conscious use of those forms of struggle of the revolutionary classes which arise spontaneously in the course of the movement. Marxism, absolutely hostile to all abstract formulas, to all doctrinaire recipes, demands that the most careful attention should be paid to the proceeding *mass* struggle, which, as the movement develops, as the consciousness of the masses grows, and as economic and political crises become increasingly acute, gives rise to new and varied defensive and offensive methods. Marxism, therefore, does not repudiate any form of struggle. Marxism in no wise confines itself to the forms of struggle that are possible and that are practiced at any particular moment; it realizes that new forms of struggle, unknown at the given period, must *inevitably* arise as the given social situation changes. In this respect Marxism *learns,* if one may so express it, from the practice of the masses, and is far from claiming to *teach* the masses forms of struggle invented by arm-chair "systematizers." Kautsky, for instance, when examining the forms of the social revolution, said – We know that the next crisis will develop new forms of struggle, although we are unable to foresee them at the present time.

In the second place, Marxism unconditionally demands that the question of the forms of struggle should be examined *historically.* He who considers this question without relation to the concrete historical situation, does not even understand the ABC of dialectical materialism. At different moments of economic evolution, and depending on varying political, national, cultural, and other social conditions, different forms of struggle assume prominence, become the chief forms of struggle, whereupon, in their turn, the secondary and supplementary forms of struggle also change their aspect. He who endeavors to accept or reject a definite means of struggle without a detailed examination of the concrete conditions of the given moment at the given stage of its development, has entirely abandoned Marxist ground.

These are the two main theoretical principles by which we must be guided. The history of Marxism in Western Europe provides infinite examples in confirmation of what has been said. The European Social-Democrats at the present time regard parliamentarism and the trade union movement as the principal forms of struggle; they recognized insurrection in the past and are quite prepared to recognize it in the future if conditions change – despite the opinion of the liberal bourgeoisie of the type of the Russian Cadets and the adherents of *Bez Zaglavia.*[*] The Social-

---

[*] Name of the paper *Bez Zaglavia,* issued in 1906 by Prokopovich and

Democrats in the 'seventies rejected the general strike as a social panacea, as a means of immediately overthrowing the bourgeoisie by non-political methods: but the Social-Democrats (particularly after the experience in Russia in 1905), entirely accept the mass political strike as *one* method of struggle which is essential under *certain* conditions. The Social-Democrats were in favor of street barricade fighting in the 'forties, rejected it for definite reasons at the end of the nineteenth century, and expressed their entire readiness to revise this view and to admit the expediency of barricade warfare after the experience in Moscow had given rise, in the words of K. Kautsky, to new barricade tactics.

V. I. Lenin, *Collected Works,* Russian edition, Vol. X, pp. 80-81.

The methods of conducting warfare, the forms of warfare, are not always the same. They change in accordance with the conditions of development, and primarily of the development of production. In the time of Genghis Khan war was not waged in the same way as it was waged in the time of Napoleon III; in the twentieth century it is not waged in the way it was waged in the nineteenth century.

The art of warfare under modern conditions consists in mastering all forms of fighting and all the achievements of science in this sphere, utilizing them intelligently, combining them intelligently, or making timely use of one or another of these forms as the circumstances of the situation require.

The same applies to the forms of struggle in the political sphere. The forms of struggle in the political sphere are even more varied than the forms of warfare. They change with the development of economic life, social life, and culture, with the condition of classes, the relation of the contending forces, the nature of government and, finally with international relations. The illegal form of struggle under absolutism, combined with partial strikes and workers' demonstrations; the open form of struggle, when "legal opportunities" existed, and mass political strikes of the workers; the par-

---

Kuskova, the one-time authors of the "Credo," the earliest Russian expression of revisionism. The adherents of *Bez Zaglavia* professed "critical socialism," but were in fact even more Right than the West European revisionists, almost approximating to the Cadets in their reformist policy. – *Ed.*

liamentary form of struggle at the time, say, of the Duma and extra-parliamentary demonstrations of the masses at times assuming the character of armed insurrections; lastly, state forms of struggle, when the proletariat had taken power and is able to utilize all the means and forces of the state, including the army – such in general are the forms of struggle which were developed in the practice of the revolutionary struggle of the proletariat. It is the duty of the Party to master these forms of struggle, to combine them intelligently on the field of combat, and skillfully to direct the struggle into such forms as are particularly expedient in the given situation.

The forms of organization of armies and the kinds of troops are usually adapted to the forms and methods of conducting warfare. The former change with the latter. In a war of maneuvers the issue is frequently decided by massed cavalry. In trench warfare, on the other hand, the cavalry plays either no part at all, or a subordinate part; artillery and aviation, gas and tanks, then decide everything.

The aim of the art of warfare is to utilize all the various kinds of troops, to perfect them and to skillfully combine their operations.

The same is true of the forms of organization in the political sphere. Here, as in the military sphere, the forms of organization are adapted to the forms of struggle. Secret organizations of professional revolutionaries in the era of absolutism; educational, trade union, cooperative and parliamentary organizations (the fractions in the Duma, etc.) in the era of the Duma; factory and workshop committees, peasant committees, strike committees, Soviets of workers' and soldiers' deputies, revolutionary military committees, and a large proletarian party uniting all these forms of organization, during the period of mass action and insurrection; finally, the state form of organization of the proletariat when the power of government becomes concentrated in the hands of the working class – such in general are the forms of organization which, under varying conditions, the proletariat can and must utilize in its struggle against the bourgeoisie.

It is the duty of the Party to master all these forms of organization, perfect them and skillfully combine their work at each particular moment.

Joseph Stalin, "Strategy and Tactics of the Russian Communists," *Pravda,* 1923, No. 56.

III. STRATEGIC AND TACTICAL BOLSHEVIK LEADERSHIP

1. Leadership – Strategic and Fundamental

A. Strategic Leadership

...The reserves of the revolution can be:

Direct: (a) the peasantry and in general the intermediate strata of the population within the country; (b) the proletariat of the neighboring countries; (c) the revolutionary movement in the colonies and the dependent countries; (d) the gains and achievements of the dictatorship of the proletariat – part of which the proletariat may renounce temporarily, while retaining superiority of forces, in order to buy off a powerful enemy and thus gain a respite; and *Indirect:* (a) the contradictions and conflicts between the non-proletarian classes within the country that can be utilized by the proletariat to weaken the enemy or to strengthen its own reserves; (b) contradictions, conflicts and wars (the imperialist war, for instance) between bourgeois states inimical to the proletarian state which can be utilized by the proletariat in its offensive or in maneuvering in the event of a forced retreat.

There is no need to speak at length about the reserves of the first category, as their significance is understood by every one. As for the reserves of the second category, the significance of which is not always clear, it must be said that sometimes they become of prime importance for the course of the revolution. For instance, the supreme importance of the conflict between the petty-bourgeois democrats (Socialist-Revolutionaries) and the liberal-monarchist bourgeoisie (the Cadets) during the first revolution and afterwards, can hardly be denied, for it undoubtedly played its part in the liberation of the peasantry from the influence of the bourgeoisie. Still less grounds are there for denying the tremendous importance of the fact that the principal groups of imperialists were engaged in mortal combat among themselves at the time of the October Revolution, when the imperialists busy with their internecine strife were not in a position to concentrate their forces against the young Soviet power, for which very reason the proletariat was able to devote its entire attention to the organization of its forces and the fortification of its power, and to prepare for the rout of Kolchak and Denikin. We must therefore, assume that now, when the contradictions between the imperialist groups are becoming more and more profound, when a new war among them is becoming inevitable, reserves of this description will become more and more important for the proletariat.

The task of strategic leadership is to utilize properly all these reserves for the achievement of the basic aims of the revolution at a given stage of its development.

What does proper utilization of the reserves mean?

It means complying with several necessary conditions of which the following must be regarded as the principal ones:

First: the concentration of the main forces of the revolution at the decisive moment at the most vulnerable point of the enemy, when the revolution has already become ripe, when the offensive is in full swing, when insurrection knocks at the door and when the moving up of reserves to the vanguard is the decisive condition of success. The strategy of the Party, during the period April to October 1917, well illustrates this manner of utilizing reserves. At that time the most vulnerable point of the enemy was undoubtedly the war. It was undoubtedly on this very question, a fundamental one, that the Party rallied the broadest masses of the population around the proletarian vanguard. The strategy of the Party during that period was, while training the vanguard in street action by means of demonstrations, etc., to bring up the reserves to the vanguard by means of the soviets in the rear and the soldiers' committees at the front. The outcome of the revolution has shown that proper use was made of the reserves.

This is what Lenin, paraphrasing the well-known theses of Marx and Engels on insurrection, says about this condition of the strategic utilization of the forces of the revolution:

> Never *play* with insurrection; but, when it is once begun, know firmly that it must be *carried through to the end.* Concentrate, at the decisive place and time, *forces greatly superior* to those of the enemy; otherwise the latter, better prepared and better organized, will destroy the insurgents. Once the insurrection has begun, it is necessary to act with the greatest *determination,* and, at all costs, *on the offensive.* The defensive is the death of every armed rising. Make sure of taking the enemy by surprise, and seize the moment when his troops are scattered. Endeavour to win successes *each day,* even small ones (one might say each hour in the case of one town), and at all costs maintain

moral ascendancy. (*Collected Works,* Vol. XXI, Book 2, pp. 97-98.)

Second: the selection of the moment for striking the decisive blow, the moment for initiating the insurrection so timed as to co-incide with the moment when the crisis has attained its highest pitch, when the preparedness of the vanguard to fight it out to the end, the preparedness of the reserves to support the vanguard and when the maximum consternation in the ranks of the enemy are evident.

> "The decisive battle," says Lenin, may be deemed to be fully matured *when* "all the class forces hostile to us have become sufficiently confused, are sufficiently at loggerheads with each other, have sufficiently weakened themselves in a struggle beyond their capacities"; *when* "all the vacillating, wavering, unstable, intermediate elements – the petty bour-geoisie and the petty-bourgeois democrats, as distinct from the bourgeoisie – have sufficiently exposed themselves be-fore the people, and have sufficiently disgraced themselves through their practical bankruptcy"; *when* "among the prole-tariat a mass mood in favor of supporting the most deter-mined, unreservedly bold, revolutionary action against the bourgeoisie has arisen and begins to grow powerfully. Then indeed, revolution is ripe; then, indeed, if we have correctly gauged all the conditions outlined above, and if we have chosen the moment rightly, our victory is assured." (*"Left-Wing" Communism, etc.,* pp. 93-94.)

The manner in which the October insurrection was carried out may be taken as a model of such strategy.

Failure to observe this condition leads to a dangerous error called "loss of tempo," as when the Party lags behind the course of the movement or runs far ahead of it, courting the danger of failure. An example of this "loss of tempo," of the inopportune choice of the moment of insurrection, may be seen in the attempt made by a section of our comrades to begin an uprising with the arrest of the Democratic Conference in August 1917, when hesitation was still rife in the soviets, when the front was still at the crossroads and the reserves had not yet been brought up to the vanguard.

Third: a course having been mapped out, it must be pursued no matter what difficulties and complications may be encountered on the road. This is necessary so that the vanguard may not lose sight of the main aim of the struggle and the masses may not stray from the road while marching to that goal and attempting to rally around the vanguard. Disregard of this condition leads to a grievous error well known to sailors as "losing the course." As an example of this "loss of course" we may mention the mistaken conduct of our Party immediately after the Democratic Conference when it (the Party) adopted a resolution to participate in the Preliminary Parliament. For the moment the Party seemed to have forgotten that the Preliminary Parliament represented an attempt of the bourgeoisie to lead the country away from the path of the soviets to the path of bourgeois parliamentarism, that participation by the Party in any such body might result in a reshuffling of all the cards and mislead the workers and peasants who were waging a revolutionary struggle under the slogan: "All Power to the Soviets." This error was corrected by the withdrawal of the Bolsheviks from the Preliminary Parliament.

Fourth: maneuvering with the reserves calculated to effect a correct retreat when the enemy is strong, when retreat is inevitable, when the disadvantages of engaging in a battle forced upon us by the enemy are obvious, when retreat is the only way under the given alignment of forces to ward off a blow from the vanguard and keep the reserves intact.

> The revolutionary parties (says Lenin) must complete their education. They have learned to attack. Now they must understand that it is necessary to supplement this knowledge with the knowledge of how to retreat properly. They must understand – and the revolutionary class by its own bitter experience learns to understand – that victory is impossible without having learned both how to attack and how to retreat correctly. (*"Left-Wing" Communism, etc.,* p. 21.)

The object of this strategy is to gain time, to disintegrate the enemy and to accumulate forces in order to assume the offensive later.

The signing of the Brest-Litovsk Peace may be taken as a model of this strategy, for it enabled the Party to gain time, to make use of the clashes in the camps of the imperialists, to disintegrate the forces of the enemy, to retain the support of the peasantry and accumulate forces in preparation for the attacks upon Kolchak and Denikin.

"In concluding a separate peace," said Lenin at that time, "we free ourselves as far as possible at the present moment from both groups of imperialist belligerents, we take advantage of their mutual enmity and warfare which hamper concerted action on their part against us, and for a certain period have our hands free to advance and to consolidate the socialist revolution." (*Collected Works*, Russian edition, Vol. XXII, p. 198.)

"Now even the biggest fool," said Lenin, three years after the Brest-Litovsk Peace, "can see that the Brest-Litovsk Peace was a concession that strengthened us and broke up the forces of international imperialism." (*Collected Works*, Russian edition, Vol. XXVII, p. 7.)

These are the principal conditions underlying correct strategic direction.

Joseph Stalin, *Leninism*, Vol. I, pp. 76-80.

B. Maneuvering Reserves, Retreat and Advance in the Class Struggle of the Proletariat

If an army, when it had become convinced that it was unable to take a fortress by storm, declared that it refused to abandon the old positions and occupy new positions and that it would not adopt new methods to gain its objective, of such an army it might be said that he who has learned to attack but has not learned to adapt himself to certain difficult conditions, will never win a war. History knows no wars, or only as rare exceptions, which uniformly began and ended by a triumphant advance. That applies to ordinary wars. As to the kind of a war that decides the fate of a class, decides whether there should be capitalism or socialism – is there any reasonable ground for assuming that a people which is attacking this problem for the first time will at once discover the only correct and infallible solution? What grounds are there for assuming this? None at all. Experience, in fact, goes to prove the contrary. There was not a single problem among those we solved which did not demand a second solution, which did not require to be tackled a second time. Having suffered defeat, to start once again, to do everything over once more, to learn how the problem can be tackled, to learn how the solution of the problem can be approached, not a final and correct solution, but, at least, a satisfactory solution – that is the way we worked, and that is the way we must continue to work. If, in view of the prospect which is now opening before us, there were no unanimity in our ranks, it would be a deplorable sign that an extremely dangerous spirit of despondency had infected our Party. And, on the contrary, if we do not fear to speak the most bitter and painful truths openly we shall learn, unfailingly and certainly learn, to overcome each and every difficulty.

We must base ourselves on existing capitalist relations. Does that task dismay us? Or shall we say that the task is not a communist one? That would mean failure to understand the revolutionary struggle, failure to understand the character of that struggle, which is an extremely tense struggle, liable to the most abrupt changes which we must under no possible circumstances ignore.

V. I. Lenin, *Collected Works,* Russian edition, Vol. XXVII, pp. 69-70.

...When it was necessary – in accordance with the objective state of affairs prevailing in Russia and the world generally – to move forward, to attack the enemy with supreme courage, dash and determination, we attacked. When necessary, we shall do so again and again.

In this way we raised our revolution to a level the world has never known. No force in the world, no matter what evil, misfortune and torment it may bring to millions and hundreds of millions of people, can deprive us of the main achievements of our revolution, because they are no longer "our" achievements, but the achievements of world history.

And when, in the spring of 1921, it appeared that the vanguard of our revolution ran the risk of becoming divorced from the mass of the people, from the mass of the peasantry, which it was its duty to lead forward intelligently, we unanimously and resolutely decided to retreat. And during the past year we have on the whole retreated in orderly revolutionary fashion.

The revolutions of the proletariat which are ripening in all the advanced countries of the world will not achieve their aims unless they combine the ability to fight and to attack self-sacrificingly with the ability to retreat in revolutionary order. The experience gained in the second phase of our struggle, *i.e.,* the experience in retreating, will also, most likely, be of value in the future to the workers of at least certain countries, and just as the experience we gained in the first phase of the revolution, the experience in supremely courageous attack, will be of undoubted value to the workers of all countries.

We have now decided to consider the retreat ended.

This means that all the aims of our policy are to be reconsidered from a new aspect.

The important thing now is that the vanguard shall not hesitate to educate itself, to remold itself, openly to admit that its training and abilities are inadequate. The whole point now is to advance in incomparably wider and more powerful masses, but not otherwise than together with the peasantry, demonstrating to the peasantry in deed, in practice, by experience, that we are learning, and will learn to help them and to lead them forward.

V. I. Lenin, *Collected Works,* Russian edition, Vol. XXVII, p. 271.

...An advance *without consolidating* the positions already captured is an advance doomed to failure. When can an advance be successful, in the military sphere, let us say? When the advancing force does not confine itself simply to moving forward headlong, but tries at the same time to *consolidate* the positions captured, to *regroup* its forces in accordance with the changed circumstances, to strengthen the rear and to bring up reserves. Why is all that necessary? As a protection against surprises, in order to close up possible breaches in the line of attack, which may happen in every advance, and thus to prepare for the complete liquidation of the enemy. The mistake that the Polish armies made in 1920, if we take only the military side of the matter, was that they ignored this rule. That, among other reasons, is why, having advanced headlong to Kiev, they were obliged to retreat in a no less headlong manner to Warsaw. The mistake the Soviet forces made in 1920, again if we take only the military side of the question, was that, in their advance on Warsaw, they repeated the error committed by the Poles.

The same is true of the laws of advance on the front of the class struggle. It is impossible to conduct a successful advance with the purpose of liquidating the class enemies, *without consolidating* the positions already captured, without *regrouping* the forces, without supplying the front with *reserves* and without bringing up the *rear*, etc.

The whole point of the matter is that the muddle-heads do not understand the laws of advance. The whole point of the matter is that the Party *does* understand them and carries them out in practice.

...They do not understand the class nature of the attack. They talk loudly about attack. But an attack on *which* class, and in alliance with *which* class? We are conducting an attack on the capitalist elements of the countryside in alliance with the middle peasant, for only such an attack can assure us victory. But what is to be done when, in their onrush, certain sections of the Party begin to divert the attack from its right direction and to turn its edge against our ally, against the middle peasant? Is it *any kind* of attack we want, and not an attack against a definite class, in alliance with a definite class? Don Quixote also imagined he was attacking enemies when he attacked windmills. But we know that he only got a bruised head from this apology for an attack.

Joseph Stalin, *Leninism,* Vol. II, pp. 235-36.

...Some comrades think that the main thing in the socialist offensive is repressions, and if repressions don't increase there is no offensive. Is this true? Of course it is untrue.

Repressions are a necessary element in the offensive, but an auxiliary, not a principal element. The principal element in the socialist offensive, in present conditions, consists in increasing the rate of development of our industry, increasing the rate of development of the soviet farms and collective farms, increasing the rate of the economic squeezing out of the capitalist elements in town and country, mobilizing the masses around the cause of socialist construction, mobilizing the masses against capitalism. You may arrest and exile tens and hundreds of thousands of kulaks, but if at the same time you do not do everything necessary to hasten the building of new forms of economy, replace the old capitalist forms of economy by new forms, blow up and liquidate the productive sources of the economic existence and development of the capitalist elements in the countryside – the kulaks will be reborn and grow just the same.

Others think that the socialist offensive is a headlong march forward, without proper preparation, without regrouping of forces in the course of offensive, without consolidating the positions occupied, without utilizing reserves to develop our successes, and, if symptoms have appeared of, say, an ebb of a part of the peasantry away from the collective farms, this means that we already have "the ebb tide of the revolution," a decline in the movement, a check to the offensive.

Is this true? Of course it is untrue.

In the first place not a single offensive, be it ever so successful, takes place without some breaks and overhastiness on individual sections of the front. To argue, because of this, that the offensive has been checked, or that it has collapsed shows that the essence of the offensive has not been understood.

Secondly, there has never been, and can never be a *successful* offensive without a regrouping of forces in the course of the offensive itself, without consolidating the occupied positions, without utilizing reserves to develop successes and push the offensive to its conclusion. In a headlong movement, *i.e.,* one that does not observe these conditions, the offensive must inevitably work itself to a standstill and collapse. Rushing forward headlong is fatal in an offensive. Our rich experience in the civil war teaches us this.

Joseph Stalin, *Leninism,* Vol. II, pp. 299-300.

2. Tactical Leadership

A. The Task of Tactical Leadership

Tactical leadership is a part of strategic leadership, subordinated to the tasks and the requirements of the latter. The task of tactical leadership is to master all the forms of struggle and of organization of the proletariat and to assure their correct utilization in order to achieve the maximum results obtainable with the relative strength of forces available, the maximum necessary in preparing for strategic success.

What does the correct utilization of the forms of struggle and of organization of the proletariat mean?

It means fulfilling several necessary conditions of which the following may be considered the principal ones:

First: To bring to the forefront those forms of struggle and of organization which are best suited to the conditions prevailing during the ebb or flow of the movement, as the case may be, and, therefore, calculated to facilitate and assure the bringing of the masses to the revolutionary positions, the bringing of millions to the revolutionary front and their assignment to various sectors of the revolutionary front.

The point here is not that the vanguard shall realize the impossibility of preserving the old order of things and the inevitability of its overthrow. The point is that the masses, the vast masses, shall understand this inevitability and display their readiness to support the vanguard. But the masses can understand this only through their own experiences. The task is to enable the vast masses to understand from their own experiences the inevitability of the overthrow of the old regime, to bring into being such methods of struggle and forms of organization as will make it easier for the masses to learn from their own experiences the correctness of the revolutionary slogans.

The vanguard would have become detached from the working class and the working class would have lost contact with the mass, if the Party had not decided at the time to participate in the Duma and if it had not decided to concentrate its forces on work in the Duma and to carry on the struggle on the basis of this work in order to enable the masses the more easily to see from their own experiences the futility of the Duma, the falsity of the Cadet promises, the impossibility of compromise with tsarism and the inevitability of an alliance between the peasantry and the working class. Had these experiences not been imparted to the masses during the period of the Duma, the exposure of the Cadets and the hegemony of the proletariat would have been impossible.

The danger of the "otzovist"[*] tactics consisted in that they threatened to isolate the vanguard from the reserve, numbering millions.

The Party would have been isolated from the working class and the working class would have lost its influence among the broad masses of the peasants and soldiers if the proletariat had followed in the footsteps of the "Left" Communists who called for insurrection in April 1917, when the Mensheviks and the Socialist-Revolutionaries had not yet exposed themselves as advocates of war and of imperialism, and when the masses had not yet had sufficient time to learn from their own experience how false the speeches of the Mensheviks and the Socialist-Revolutionaries about peace,

---

[*] From the Russian *otosvat* – to recall, the name given to a group of Bolsheviks which advocated the recall of the Social-Democratic deputies from the Duma. – *Ed.*

land and freedom were. Had it not been for the experiences the masses gained during the Kerensky period, the Mensheviks and Socialist-Revolutionaries would not have become isolated and the dictatorship of the proletariat would have been impossible. Therefore, the tactic of "patiently explaining" the mistakes of the petty-bourgeois parties and of open struggle in the soviets was the only correct tactic.

The danger of the tactics of the "Left" Communists was that they threatened to reduce the Party from the position of leader of the proletarian revolution, to that of a band of inane conspirators with no contacts with the masses.

> With the vanguard alone, victory is impossible (says Lenin). To throw the vanguard alone into the decisive battle before the whole class, before the broad masses have taken up a position either of direct support of the vanguard, or at least of benevolent neutrality toward it... would not merely be folly but a crime. And in order that actually the whole class, that actually the broad masses of toilers and those oppressed by capital may take up such a position, propaganda and agitation alone are not sufficient. For this, the masses must have their own political experience. Such is the fundamental law of all great revolutions, confirmed now with astonishing force and vividness not only in Russia but also in Germany. It has been necessary – not only for the uncultured, often illiterate masses of Russia but for the highly cultured, entirely literate masses of Germany – to realize through their own painful experience the absolute impotence and characterlessness, the absolute helplessness and servility before the bourgeoisie, the absolute baseness of the government of the knights of the Second International, the absolute inevitability of a dictatorship of the extreme reactionaries (Kornilov in Russia, Kapp and Co. in Germany) as the only alternatives to a dictatorship of the proletariat, in order to turn them resolutely toward Communism. (*"Left-Wing" Communism, etc.*, pp. 72-73.)

Second: To locate at any given moment that single link in the chain of events which, if seized upon, will enable us to keep hold of the whole chain and prepare the ground for the achievement of strategic success.

37

The point here is to single out from the tasks confronting the Party precisely the one that must be fulfilled next, the fulfillment of which is the central point and which will assure the successful fulfillment of the remaining urgent tasks.

The importance of this postulate may be illustrated by two examples, one of which may be taken from the remote past (the period of the formation of the Party) and the other from the immediate present (the period of the New Economic Policy).

In the period of the formation of the Party, when the multiplicity of circles and organizations had not yet been linked together, when primitive methods and small circles were disintegrating the Party from top to bottom, when ideological confusion was a characteristic feature of our inner Party life, the master link in the chain and the principal task of all the tasks then confronting the Party proved to be the establishment of an all-Russian illegal newspaper. Why? Because under the conditions then obtaining, an harmonious Party nucleus capable of uniting these innumerable circles and organizations into a single organization could be set up only through the medium of an all-Russian illegal newspaper. Only in this way could the conditions prerequisite for ideological and tactical unity be created and the ground work for the formation of a real Party be laid.

During the period of transition from war to economic construction, when industry was in a state of collapse and agriculture was suffering from a shortage of city manufactures, when the bond between state industry and peasant farming became the fundamental condition for successful socialist construction – at that time the master link in the chain of processes, the fundamental task, was to develop trade. Why? Because under the conditions of the New Economic Policy, the bond between industry and peasant agriculture could not be established otherwise than through trade, because, under N. E. P., production without sale is the death of industry; because industry can be expanded only by the expansion of sales, by the development of trade, because only after strengthening our position in the sphere of trade, only after securing control of trade, only after seizing upon this link can there be any hope of linking industry with the rural market and successfully solving other urgent problems so that the conditions necessary for building the foundations of socialist economy could be created.

It is not enough to be a revolutionary and an adherent

of socialism or of communism in general (says Lenin). What is needed is the ability to find at any moment that particular link in the chain which must be grasped with all one's might in order to gain control of the whole chain and prepare thoroughly for the passing on to the next link.... At the present time... this link is the revival of internal *trade* under correct state regulation (guidance). Commerce is the "link" in the historical chain of events, in the transitional forms of our socialist construction which we must grasp with all our might. (*Collected Works,* Russian edition, Vol. XXVII, p. 82.)

These are the main conditions which assure correct tactical leadership.

Joseph Stalin, *Leninism,* Vol. I, pp. 81-84.

B. Combining Legal and Illegal Forms of Struggle in Proletarian Tactics

Everyone will agree that an army which does not train itself to wield all arms, all means and methods of warfare that the enemy possesses or may possess, is behaving in an unwise, or even in a criminal manner. This applies to politics to a greater degree than it does to war. In politics it is harder to forecast what methods of warfare may be applicable and useful for us under certain future conditions. Unless we are able to master all methods of warfare, we stand the risk of suffering great, and sometimes decisive defeat if the changes in the position of the other classes, which are not of our making, will bring to the front forms of activity in which we are particularly weak. If, however, we are able to master all methods of warfare, we shall certainly be victorious, because we represent the interests of the really advanced, of the really revolutionary class, even if circumstances do not permit us to use weapons that are most dangerous for the enemy, weapons that are most quickly death-dealing. Inexperienced revolutionaries often think that legal methods of struggle are opportunistic because in this field the bourgeoisie particularly frequently (especially in "peaceful," non-revolutionary times) deceived and fooled the workers, and they think that illegal methods of struggle are revolutionary. But this is not true. What is true is that the opportunists and the traitors to the working class are those parties and leaders who are not able or who do not want (don't say: you cannot; say: you won't) to apply illegal methods of struggle in conditions such as those which prevailed, for example, during the imperialist war of 1914-18, when the bourgeoisie of the freest democratic countries deceived the workers in the most impudent and brutal manner and prohibited everyone from speaking the truth about the predatory character of the war. But revolutionaries who are unable to combine illegal forms of struggle with *every* form of legal struggle are very poor revolutionaries. It is not difficult to be a revolutionary when the revolution has already flared up, when everybody joins the revolution simply because he is carried away by it, because it is the fashion and sometimes even because it might open a career. After the victory the proletariat has to exert extreme effort, to suffer pains and one might say martyrdom to "liberate" itself from such alleged revolutionaries. It is much more difficult – and much more useful – to be a revolutionary when the conditions for direct, open, really mass and really revolutionary struggle do *not yet* exist, to be able to defend the interests of the revolution (by propaganda, agitation and organization) in non-revolutionary bodies and even in reactionary bodies, in non-revolutionary circumstances, among the masses who are incapable of immediately appreciating the need for revolutionary methods of action. The main task of contemporary Communism in Western Europe and America is to acquire the ability to seek, to find, to determine correctly the concrete path or the particular turn of events that will *bring* the masses *right up* to the real, decisive, last and great revolutionary struggle.

V. I. Lenin, *"Left-Wing" Communism: An Infantile Disorder,* pp. 75-76.

C. Leading the Masses into Revolutionary Positions as a Result of Their Own Political Experience – an Important Tactical Principle of Leninism

This tactical principle involves the question of changes of slogans, and of the order and method of this change. It involves the question as to how slogans for the Party are to be transformed into slogans for the masses; it involves the question as to how the masses are to be led into revolutionary positions, so that the masses may be convinced from their own political experience of the correctness of the Party slogans. For the masses cannot be convinced by propaganda and agitation alone. The political experience of the masses themselves is required for this. It is necessary that the broad masses should learn from their own personal sufferings that the overthrow of the given system, let us say, is inevitable and that the establishment of a new political and social system is inevitable. It was a good thing, for instance, that the advanced group, the Party, was already convinced of the inevitability, let us say, of the overthrow of the Milyukov-Kerensky Provisional Government in April 1917. But this was not enough to enable us to come out for the overthrow of that government, to advance the slogan of the overthrow of the Provisional Government and the establishment of the Soviet government *as a slogan of the day*. In order to convert the formula "All Power to the Soviets" from an immediate *prospect* into *a slogan of the day*, a slogan of immediate action, another decisive factor was required, namely that the masses themselves should become convinced of the correctness of this slogan, and should in one way or another assist the Party in carrying this slogan into effect. A distinction must be drawn between a formula which is an immediate *prospect* and a formula which is *a slogan of the day*. It is precisely this that the group of Bolsheviks in Petrograd headed by Comrade Bogdatyev in April 1917, failed to understand when it *prematurely* put forward the slogan, "Down with the Provisional Government, All Power to the Soviets." Lenin at that time qualified this attempt on the part of Comrade Bogdatyev as a dangerous piece of adventurism and pilloried him publicly. Why? Because the wide mass of toilers in the rear and at the front were not yet receptive to this slogan. Because this group confused the formula "All Power to the Soviets" as a prospect with the slogan "All Power to the Soviets" as a slogan of the day. Because they *ran ahead* and incurred the danger of the Party's becoming completely isolated from the masses and from the Soviets, which at that time still believed that the Provisional Government was revolutionary.

Should the Chinese Communists, for instance, six months ago, have put forward the slogan, "Down with the Kuomintang leadership in Wuchang?" No, they should not. They should not because this would be dangerously *running ahead,* it would have prevented contact between the Communists and the broad masses of toilers, who still believed in the leadership of the Kuomintang; it would have isolated the Communist Party from the peasant masses. They should not because the Wuchang Kuomintang leadership, the Wuchang Central Committee of the Kuomintang, had not yet run its course as a bourgeois revolutionary government: it had not yet disgraced and discredited itself in the eyes of the broad masses of toilers by its fight against the agrarian revolution, its fight against the working class and its swing-over to counter-revolution. We always said that it was impossible to adopt the policy of discrediting and replacing the Wuchang Kuomintang leadership before it had run its course as a bourgeois revolutionary government, and that it must first be allowed to run its course before practically raising the question of replacing it. Should the Chinese Communists put forward the slogan, "Down with the Kuomintang leadership in Wuchang" now? Yes, they should, unconditionally. Now that the Kuomintang leadership has already disgraced itself by its fight against the revolution, now that it has adopted a hostile attitude to the workers and peasant masses, this slogan will meet with a powerful response on the part of the mass of the people. Every worker and every peasant will now realize that the Communists were right in withdrawing from the Wuchang government and from the Wuchang Central Committee of the Kuomintang, and in putting forward the slogan, "Down with the Kuomintang leadership in Wuchang." For the peasant and worker masses are now faced with the alternative: *either* the present leadership of the Kuomintang, which means that there will be no hope of satisfying the urgent needs of these masses and that the agrarian revolution will be abandoned; *or* an agrarian revolution and a radical improvement of the condition of the working class, and then the removal of the Kuomintang leadership in Wuchang will become a slogan of the day for the masses.

Such are the demands of the third tactical principle of Leninism in connection with the question of changes of slogans, of the ways and means of bringing the masses to new revolutionary positions and of how, by one's policy and actions, and by a *timely* change of slogans, to help the broad masses of toilers to realize from their own experience the correctness of the line of the Party.

Joseph Stalin, *The Opposition,* pp. 627-29.

D. Selection of the Chief Link in the Chain – a Principle of Tactical Leadership

Political events are always highly entangled and complicated. They may be compared with a chain: If you want to lay hold of the whole chain, you must not seize only one link. You cannot artificially choose the link you wish to seize hold of. What was the crux of the situation in 1917? It was to get out of the war; this is what all the people were demanding and it covered everything. Revolutionary Russia got out of the war. It required a great effort, but as a result the essential need of the people was taken into consideration, and that insured us victory for many years ahead.... And the people felt, the peasants saw, every soldier returning from the front perfectly understood that in the shape of the Soviet government he was obtaining a more democratic government, a government that was closer to the toilers. No matter what foolish and outrageous things we might do in other spheres, we had respected this main desire, and therefore, everything we did was right.

What was the crux of the situation in 1919 and 1920? It was to offer military resistance. We were being attacked and stifled by the world-powerful Entente. And no propaganda was necessary – any non-Party peasant understood what was going on. The landlord was attacking. The Communists knew how to fight him. That is why the masses of the peasants were on the side of the Communists; that is why we were victorious.

In 1921 the crux of the situation was to retreat in good order. That is why we needed strict discipline. The "Workers' Opposition" said: "You are underestimating the workers, the workers must display greater initiative." But initiative must consist in retreating in good order and preserving strict discipline. Whoever introduced the slightest note of panic or was guilty of the slightest violation of discipline would have ruined the revolution; because nothing is more difficult than to retreat with people who have been accustomed to victory, who are imbued with revolutionary views and ideals, and who in their heart of hearts regard every retreat as an infamy. The greatest danger, lies in violating good order, and the greatest task is to preserve good order.

And what is the crux of the situation now? The crux of the situation – and with this I would like to sum up my report – does not lie in the sphere of politics, in the sense of a change of direction. About this there is much too much talk in connection with the New Economic Policy. This is to no purpose. It is dangerous talk. People are beginning to create a great deal of pother in connection with the New Economic Policy, to reorganize institutions and to form new institutions. It is dangerous talk. What we have come to is this, that the key to the situation lies in people, the selection of people. That is hard to understand for a revolutionary who is accustomed to resist preoccupation with petty matters, with dabbling in culture; and now instead of the reorganization of institutions, must stress the role of the individual. But we have arrived at a situation which politically must be soberly weighed – we have advanced so far ahead that we cannot retain all our positions, and we must not do so.

V. I. Lenin, *Collected Works,* Russian edition, Vol. XXVII, pp. 254-55.

3. The Importance of Slogans in Strategy and Tactics

Skillfully formulated decisions expressing the aims of the war or of individual engagements, and popular among the troops, are sometimes of paramount importance at the front in inspiring the army to action, in maintaining its spirit, and so forth. Proper orders, slogans, or appeals to the troops are as important to the success of the war as first-class heavy artillery or first-class fast tanks.

Still more important are slogans in the political sphere, where one has to deal with vast numbers of the population, with their various demands and requirements.

A slogan is a brief and clear formulation of the aims of the struggle, near or remote, given by the leading group, let us say, of the proletariat, its party. Slogans vary in accordance with the different aims of the struggle, which embrace either a whole historical period or individual phases and episodes of the given historical period. The slogan, "Down with the Autocracy," which was first put forward by the *Group for the Emancipation of Labor* in the 'eighties of the last century, was a *propagandist* slogan since its aim was to win over to the Party individuals and groups of the more steadfast and sturdy fighters. During the Russo-Japanese War, when the instability of the autocracy became more or less apparent to large sections of the working class, this slogan became an *agitational* slogan, for it was designed to win over large masses of the toilers. In the period just prior to the February 1917 Revolution, when tsarism had already completely discredited itself in the eyes of the masses, the slogan, "Down with the Autocracy" was transformed from an agitational slogan into a slogan of *action,* since it was designed to move vast masses to attack tsarism. During the February Revolution this slogan became a Party *directive,* in other words, it became a direct call to seize definite institutions and definite positions of the tsarist system, for it was already a question of overthrowing and destroying tsarism. A directive is a direct call to action by the Party, to act at a certain time and in a certain place, which is obligatory upon all members of the Party and, if the call properly and aptly formulates the demands of the masses, and if it is really ripe, it is usually taken up by large masses of toilers.

To confuse slogans with directives, or an agitational slogan with a slogan of action, is dangerous; just as premature or belated action is dangerous and sometimes even fatal. In April 1917, the slogan, "All Power to the Soviets" was an *agitational* slogan. The well-known demonstration which took place in Petrograd in April 1917 under the slogan, "All Power to the Soviets," and which surrounded the Winter Palace, was an attempt, a premature and therefore fatal attempt, to convert the slogan into a slogan of *action*. This was a very dangerous example of the misinterpretation of an agitational slogan as a slogan of action. The Party was right when it condemned the initiators of this demonstration, for it knew that the conditions had not yet arrived which would make the transformation of this slogan into a slogan of action possible, and that premature action on the part of the proletariat might result in the destruction of its forces.

On the other hand, there are times when the Party must, within twenty-four hours, "cancel" or change a slogan (or directive) which has already been adopted and which is ripe – in order to guard its ranks against a trap set by the enemy – or to defer the fulfillment of a directive to a more favorable moment. Such a case arose in Petrograd in June 1917, when a demonstration of workers and soldiers, carefully prepared and appointed for June 9, was "suddenly" cancelled by the Central Committee of our Party owing to the fact that the situation had changed. The task of the Party is to be able skillfully and at the proper time to transform agitational slogans into slogans of action, or slogans of action into definite and concrete directives, or, if the situation demands, to display enough flexibility and determination to cancel any slogans in good time, however popular and however ripe they may be.

Joseph Stalin, "Strategy and Tactics of the Russian Communists," *Pravda,* 1923, No. 56.

IV. REVOLUTIONARY AND REFORMIST LEADERSHIP

1. The Bolshevik Attitude Toward Reforms

What is the difference between revolutionary tactics and reformist tactics?

Some are of the opinion that Leninism is opposed to reforms, opposed to compromises and to agreements in general. That is absolutely untrue. Bolsheviks know as well as anybody else that in a certain sense "every little bit helps," that under certain conditions reforms, in general, and compromises and agreements, in particular, are necessary and useful.

> To carry on a war for the overthrow of the international bourgeoisie (says Lenin), a war which is a hundred times more difficult, prolonged and complicated than the most stubborn of ordinary wars between states, and to refuse beforehand to maneuver, to utilize the conflict of interests (even though temporary) among one's enemies, to refuse to temporize and compromise with possible (even though temporary, unstable, vacillating and conditional) allies – is not this ridiculous in the extreme? Is it not as though, in the difficult ascent of an unexplored and heretofore inaccessible mountain, we were to renounce beforehand the idea that at times we might have to go in zigzags, sometimes retracing our steps, sometimes giving up the course once selected and trying various others? (*"Left-Wing" Communism, etc.,* p. 52.)

Hence, it is obvious that it is not a question of reforms or compromises and agreements, as such, but of the use that is made of reforms and compromises.

To a reformist, reforms are everything while revolutionary work is just something to talk about, a diversion. Therefore, with reformist tactics under the existing bourgeois regime, reforms inevitably serve as an instrument for strengthening that regime, an instrument that disintegrates the revolution.

To a revolutionary, on the contrary, the main thing is revolutionary work and not reforms, to him reforms are by-products of the revolution. Therefore, with revolutionary tactics under the existing bourgeois regime reforms inevitably serve as instruments that disintegrate the regime, instruments that strengthen the revolution – a stronghold for the further development of the revolutionary movement.

The revolutionary will accept a reform in order to use it as a means wherewith to link legal work with illegal work, in order to use it as a screen behind which his illegal activities for the revolutionary preparation of the masses for the overthrow of the bourgeoisie may be intensified.

This is what the revolutionary utilization of reforms and agreements in an imperialist environment means.

The reformist, on the other hand, will accept reforms as a pretext for renouncing all illegal work, to thwart the preparation of the masses for the revolution and to "rest in the shade" of reforms that have been "bestowed."

This is what reformist tactics mean.

This is the position in regard to reforms and agreements under imperialism.

The situation changes somewhat, however, after the overthrow of imperialism, under the dictatorship of the proletariat. Under certain conditions and certain circumstances, the proletarian power may find itself constrained to abandon temporarily the path of revolutionary reconstruction of the existing order and take the path of its gradual transformation, the "reformist path," as Lenin says in his well-known article *On the Importance of Gold,* a path of outflanking maneuvers, a path of reforms and concessions to the non-proletarian classes in order to disintegrate these classes, give the revolution a respite, collect its forces and prepare the conditions for a new offensive. It cannot be denied that, in a sense, this is a reformist path. But there is a fundamental difference that we must bear in mind, and that is that in this case the reform emanates from the proletarian state, that it strengthens the proletarian state, that it procures for it a necessary breathing space, that its purpose is to disintegrate, not the revolution, but the non-proletarian classes.

Under such circumstances reforms are converted into their exact opposites.

The proletarian power is able to adopt such a policy because and only because the sweep of the revolution in the preceding period was sufficiently vast and allowed sufficient leeway to permit of retreat, substituting offensive tactics by tactics of temporary retreat, of detour tactics.

Thus, while formerly, under the bourgeois regime, reforms

were a by-product of the revolution, now, under the dictatorship of the proletariat, the source of reforms is the revolutionary gains of the proletariat, the reserves accumulated in the hands of the proletariat which consist of these gains.

Joseph Stalin, *Leninism,* Vol. I, pp. 84-86.

2. Lenin on Compromises

There is in this connection the question that has frequently cropped up in literature and that is constantly cropping up in the discussions on the subject under consideration – the question of the simplicity, lucidity and "rigidity" of the slogan of boycott, and also of the direct and zigzag paths of development. The direct overthrow, or, at the worst, the weakening and incapacitating of the old government and the direct creation by the people of new organs of government, undoubtedly constitute a *direct* path, a path most advantageous to the people, but which on the other hand demands the greatest expenditure of effort. When one enjoys an overwhelming superiority of forces one can succeed by a direct frontal attack. When forces are inadequate, detours, waiting periods, zigzags, retreats, and so on and so forth, may be necessary. The path of a monarchist constitution in no way, of course, precludes revolution, the elements of which are indirectly prepared and developed *also* along this path; but this is a longer path, a zigzag path.

There runs like a red thread throughout the Menshevik literature, particularly of the year 1905 (prior to October) the charge that the Bolsheviks are "rigid," admonitions, for the benefit of the Bolsheviks, that one must take account of the zigzag manner in which history proceeds. This feature of Menshevik literature is a specimen of the type of argument that asserts that horses eat oats and that the Volga flows into the Caspian Sea – the type of argument that confuses a disputable issue by reiterations of what is indisputable. That history usually moves in zigzags, and that Marxists must make allowances for the most complex and whimsical zigzags of history, is indisputable. But this much-chewed and indisputable proposition has no relation whatsoever to the problem of how a Marxist must act when history confronts the contending forces with the necessity of deciding whether to take a direct or a zigzag path. To confine oneself at moments or periods when this occurs to arguing that history usually moves in zigzags, is to be "a man in a muffler,"[*] to lose oneself in contemplation of the truism that horses eat oats. But revolutionary periods are primarily periods in history when the clash of contending social forces decides in a comparatively brief space of time whether the country shall select for a comparatively long period of time a direct or a zigzag path of development. The necessity of making allowances for zigzags does not obviate the necessity for Marxists to be able to explain to the masses at decisive moments in their history the preferability of the direct path, to be able to help the masses in the effort to select the direct path, to issue slogans in favor of such an effort, and so forth. And, upon the *conclusion* of decisive historical battles, which determine in favor of a zigzag instead of a direct path, only hopeless philistines and absolutely obtuse pedants could sneer at those who fought to the bitter end for a direct path. This would be similar to the sneers of the German official police historians, such as Treitschke, at the revolutionary slogans and revolutionary rigidity of Marx in 1848.

The attitude of Marxists towards the zigzag course of history is, as a matter of fact, similar to their attitude towards compromise. Every zigzag of history is a compromise, a compromise between the old, which is no longer strong enough completely to reject the new, and the new, which is not yet strong enough completely to overthrow the old. Marxism does not abjure compromises; Marxism deems it necessary to resort to compromises. But this does not preclude the fact that Marxism, as a live and active historical force, energetically resists compromises. He who is unable to master this seeming contradiction does not understand the ABC of Marxism.

Engels once very vividly, lucidly, and briefly expressed the attitude of Marxism towards compromises, namely, in his articles on a manifesto by the Blanquists – the Commune refugees (1874). The Blanquists, the Commune refugees, asserted in their manifesto that they tolerated no compromises. Engels ridiculed this manifesto. The point was not, he said, to abjure compromises, *to which circumstances force us* (or to which circumstances constrain us. I must beg the reader's pardon for being obliged to quote from memory, since I have no opportunity of consulting the text). The point is

---

[*] A character in one of Chekhov's stories who was always muffled up in all weather and who on hearing of some proposed new endeavor would exclaim, "I do hope nothing bad will come of it." – *Ed.*

clearly to realize the true revolutionary aims of the proletariat and to be able to pursue these aims in each and every circumstance, throughout all zigzags and compromises.

From this point of view alone can one appreciate the simplicity, directness and lucidity of boycott as a slogan of appeal to the masses. The qualities of this slogan that we have enumerated are good not in themselves, but only insofar as the objective situation in which this slogan is applied harbors the conditions of the struggle for the selection of a direct or a zigzag path of development. In the era of the Bulygin Duma this slogan was the correct and only revolutionary slogan for the workers' party not because it was the simplest, and most direct and lucid, but because historical conditions had laid upon the workers' party the duty of participating in the fight for the simple and direct revolutionary path, as against the zigzag path of a monarchist constitution.

V. I. Lenin, *Collected Works,* Russian edition, Vol. XII, pp. 20-22, "Against Boycott," 1907.

3. Reforms Before and After the Establishment of the Dictatorship of the Proletariat

Marxism alone has given a precise and correct definition of the relation between reforms and revolution, although Marx could discern this relation only from one aspect, namely, from the aspect of a situation that was antecedent to the first victory, in any way durable and in any way lasting, of the proletariat, even though obtained in one country only. In such circumstances the basis of a correct attitude was that reforms are a by-product of the revolutionary class struggle of the proletariat. This attitude is the foundation of the revolutionary tactics of the proletariat all over the capitalist world; it is an elementary truth, which is being distorted and obscured by the venal leaders of the Second International and the semi-pedantic, semi-finical knights of the Two-and-a-half International. After the proletariat has been victorious, even though in one single country, the relation between reforms and revolution acquires a new aspect. The principles remain the same, but the form undergoes a change; this Marx personally could not foresee, but it can be perceived only from the standpoint of the philosophy and policy of Marxism. Why were we able properly to carry out the Brest-Litovsk retreat? Because we had advanced so far that we had room for a retreat. We had built up the Soviet State, emerged from the imperialist war in a revolutionary way and completed the bour-geois-democratic revolution with such dizzying speed – *within the few weeks* that elapsed between October 25, 1917, and the Brest Peace – that *even* the tremendous retreat of the movement (the Brest Peace) left us with enough positions to enable us to utilize the "respite" and to march triumphantly forward against Kolchak, Denikin, Yudenich, Pilsudsky and Wrangel.

Before the victory of the proletariat, reforms are a by-product of the revolutionary class struggle. After the victory (while on an international scale they still remain "by-products"), they also become for the country which has achieved this victory a necessary and legitimate respite in cases when, after the maximum straining of the forces, the latter are patently inadequate for the revolutionary accomplishment of a particular transition. Victory creates such a "reserve strength" that it is possible to hold out even in case of an enforced retreat – to hold out materially and morally. Holding out materially means retaining a sufficient superiority of forces to prevent the enemy from smashing us completely. Holding out morally means not allowing ourselves to be demoralized and disorganized, it means retaining a sober estimate of the situation, preserving our courage and firmness of spirit, it means retreating far perhaps, but within measure, and retreating in such a way as to be able to call a halt to the retreat at the proper moment and again assume the offensive.

We retreated to state capitalism. But we retreated within meas-ure. We are now retreating to the state regulation of trade. But we are retreating within measure. There are already signs that the re-treat is coming to an end, there are signs of a possibility of calling a halt to this retreat in the not very remote future. The less prejudice we display and the more consciously, the more unanimously we accomplish this necessary retreat, the sooner will it be possible to call a halt to it, and the more certain, swift, and extensive will be our triumphant advance.

V. I. Lenin, *Collected Works,* Russian edition, Vol. XXVII, pp. 84-85.

V. PRINCIPAL TASKS OF THE STRATEGY AND TACTICS OF THE COMINTERN

1. The Fight to Win the Majority of the Working Class and Gain for It the Hegemony Over the Toiling Masses

The successful struggle of the Communist International for the dictatorship of the proletariat presupposes the existence in every country of a compact Communist Party, hardened in the struggle, disciplined, centralized, and closely linked up with the masses.

The Party is the vanguard of the working class, and consists of the best, most class-conscious, most active and most courageous members. It incorporates the whole body of experience of the proletarian struggle. Basing itself upon the revolutionary theory of Marxism and representing the general and lasting interests of the whole of the working class, the Party personifies the unity of proletarian principles, of proletarian will and of proletarian revolutionary action. It is a revolutionary organization, bound by iron discipline and strict revolutionary rules of democratic centralism, which can be carried out owing to the class-consciousness of the proletarian vanguard, to its loyalty to the revolution, its ability to maintain inseparable ties with the proletarian masses and to its correct political leadership which is constantly verified and clarified by the experiences of the masses themselves.

In order that it may fulfill its historic mission of achieving the dictatorship of the proletariat, the Communist Party must first of all set itself to accomplish the following fundamental *strategic* aims:

Extend its influence over the majority of the members of its own class, including working women and the working youth. To achieve this the Communist Party must secure predominant influence in the broad mass proletarian organizations (Soviets, trade unions, factory councils, cooperative societies, sport organizations, cultural organizations, etc.). It is particularly important for the purpose of winning over the majority of the proletariat, to capture the *trade unions,* which are genuine mass working-class organizations closely bound up with the every-day struggles of the working class. To work in reactionary trade unions and skillfully to capture them, to win the confidence of the broad masses of the industrially organized workers, to relieve and remove from their posts the reformist leaders, represent important tasks in the preparatory period.

The achievement of the dictatorship of the proletariat presupposes also that the proletariat acquires leadership of *wide sections of the toiling masses.* To accomplish this the Communist Party must extend its influence over the masses of the urban and rural poor, over the lower strata of the intelligentsia, and over the so-called "small men," *i.e.,* the petty-bourgeois strata generally. It is particularly important that work be carried on for the Party's influence over the *peasantry.* The Communist Party must secure for itself the wholehearted support of that stratum of the rural population that stands closest to the proletariat, *i.e.,* the agricultural laborers and the rural poor. To this end the agricultural laborers must be organized in separate organizations; all possible support must be given them in their struggles against the rural bourgeoisie, and strenuous work must be carried on among the small allotment farmers and small peasants. In regard to the middle strata of the peasantry in developed capitalist countries, the Communist Parties must conduct a policy to secure their neutrality. The fulfillment of all these tasks by the proletariat – the champion of the interests of the whole people and the leader of the broad masses in their struggle against the oppression of finance capital – is an essential condition precedent to the victorious Communist revolution.

The tasks of the Communist International connected with the revolutionary struggle in *colonies, semi-colonies and dependencies* are extremely important strategical tasks in the world proletarian struggle. The colonial struggle presupposes that the broad masses of the working class and of the peasantry in the colonies must be won over to the banner of the revolution: but this cannot be achieved unless the closest cooperation is maintained between the proletariat in the oppressing countries and the toiling masses in the oppressed countries.

While organizing, under the banner of the proletarian dictatorship, the revolution against imperialism in the so-called civilized states, the Communist International supports every movement against imperialist violence in the colonies, semi-colonies, and dependencies themselves (for example, Latin-America); it carries on propaganda against all forms of chauvinism and against the imperialist maltreatment of enslaved peoples and races, big and small (treatment of Negroes, "yellow labor," anti-Semitism, etc.), and supports the struggles of the latter against the bourgeoisie of the oppressing nations.

The Communist Parties in the *imperialist countries* must render systematic aid to the colonial revolutionary liberation movement, and to the movement of oppressed nationalities generally. The duty of rendering active support to these movements rests primarily upon the workers in the countries upon which the oppressed nations are economically, financially or politically dependent. The Communist Parties must openly recognize the right of the colonies to separation and their right to carry on propaganda for this separation, *i.e.,* propaganda in favor of the independence of the colonies from the imperialist state; they must recognize their right of armed defense against imperialism (*i.e.,* the right of rebellion and revolutionary war) and advocate and give active support to this defense by all the means in their power. The Communist Parties must adopt this line of policy in regard to all oppressed nations.

The Communist Parties in the *colonial and semi-colonial countries* must carry on a bold and consistent struggle against foreign imperialism and unfailingly conduct propaganda in favor of friendship and unity with the proletariat in the imperialist countries. They must openly advance, conduct propaganda for, and carry out the slogan of agrarian revolution, rouse the broad masses of the peasantry for the overthrow of the landlords and combat the reactionary and medieval influence of the priesthood, of the missionaries and other similar elements.

In these countries, the principal task is to organize the workers and the peasantry *independently* (to establish class Communist Parties of the proletariat, trade unions, peasant leagues and committees and – in a revolutionary situation – Soviets, etc.), and to free them from the influence of the national bourgeoisie, with whom temporary agreements may be made only on the condition that they, the bourgeoisie, do not hamper the revolutionary organization of the workers and peasants, and that they carry on a genuine struggle against imperialism.

Programme of the Communist International, Chapter VI, part 2.

2. Principal Tasks of the Tactics of the Comintern

In determining its line of *tactics,* each Communist Party must take into account the concrete internal and external situation, the correlation of class forces, the degree of stability and strength of the bourgeoisie, the degree of preparedness of the proletariat, the position taken up by the various intermediary strata, etc., in its country. The Party determines slogans and methods of struggle in accordance with these circumstances, with the view to organizing and mobilizing the masses on the broadest possible scale and on the highest possible level of this struggle.

When a revolutionary situation is developing, the Party advances certain transitional slogans and partial demands corresponding to the concrete situation; but these demands and slogans must be bent to the revolutionary aim of capturing power and of overthrowing bourgeois capitalist society. The Party must neither stand aloof from the daily needs and struggles of the working class nor confine its activities exclusively to them. The task of the Party is to utilize these minor everyday needs as a *starting point* from which to lead the working class to the *revolutionary struggle for power.*

When *the revolutionary tide is rising,* when the ruling classes are disorganized, the masses are in a state of revolutionary ferment, the intermediary strata are inclining towards the proletariat and the masses are ready for action and for sacrifice, the Party of the proletariat is confronted with the task of leading the masses to a direct attack upon the bourgeois state. This it does by carrying on propaganda in favor of increasingly radical transitional slogans (for soviets, workers' control of industry, for peasant committees, for the seizure of the big landed properties, for disarming the bourgeoisie and arming the proletariat, etc.), and by organizing *mass action,* upon which all branches of Party agitation and propaganda, including parliamentary activity, must be concentrated. This mass action includes: Strikes; a combination of strikes and demonstrations; a combination of strikes and armed demonstrations and finally, the general strike conjointly with armed insurrection against the state power of the bourgeoisie. The latter form of struggle, which is the supreme form, must be conducted according to the rules of war; it presupposes a plan of campaign, offensive fighting operations and unbounded devotion and heroism on the part of the proletariat. An absolutely essential condition precedent to this form of action is the organization of the broad masses into militant units, which, by their very form, embrace and set in action the largest possible numbers of toilers (Councils of Workers' and Peasants' Deputies, Soldiers' Councils, etc.), and intensified revolutionary work in the army and the navy.

In passing over to new and more radical slogans, the parties must be guided by the fundamental role of the political tactics of

Leninism, which call for ability to lead the masses to revolutionary positions in such a manner that the masses may, by their experiences, convince themselves of the correctness of the party line. Failure to observe this rule must inevitably lead to isolation from the masses, to *putschism,* to the ideological degeneration of Communism into "leftist" dogmatism, and to petty bourgeois "revolutionary" adventurism. Failure to take advantage of the culminating point in development of the revolutionary situation, when the Party of the proletariat is called upon to conduct a bold and determined attack upon the enemy, is not less dangerous. To allow that opportunity to slip by and to fail to start rebellion at that point, means to allow the initiative to pass to the enemy and to doom the revolution to defeat.

When *the revolutionary tide is not rising,* the Communist Parties must advance *partial* slogans and demands that correspond to the everyday needs of the toilers, and combine them with the fundamental tasks of the Communist International. The Communist Parties must not, however, at such a time, advance *transitional* slogans that are applicable only to revolutionary situations (for example, workers' control of industry, etc.). To advance such slogans when there is no revolutionary situation means to transform them into slogans that favor merging with the capitalist system of organization. Partial demands and slogans generally form an essential part of correct tactics; but certain transitional slogans go inseparably with a revolutionary situation. Repudiation of partial demands and transitional slogans "on principle," however, is incompatible with the tactical principles of Communism, for in effect, such repudiation condemns the Party to inaction and isolates it from the masses. *United front* tactics also occupy an important place in the tactics of the Communist Parties throughout *the whole pre-revolutionary period* as a means towards achieving success in the struggle against capital, towards the class mobilization of the masses and the exposure and isolation of the reformist leaders.

The correct application of united front tactics and the fulfillment of the general task of winning over the masses presuppose in their turn systematic and persistent work in the *trade unions* and other mass proletarian organizations. It is the bounden duty of every Communist to belong to a trade union, even a most reactionary one, provided it is a mass organization. Only by constant and persistent work in the trade unions and in the factories for the steadfast and energetic defense of the interests of the workers, together with ruthless struggle against the reformist bureaucracy, will it be possible to win the leadership in the workers' struggle and to win the industrially organized workers over to the side of the Party.

Unlike the reformists, whose policy is to split the trade unions, the Communists defend *trade union unity* nationally and internationally on the basis of the class struggle, and render every support to, and strengthen the work of, the *Red International of Labour Unions.*

In universally championing the current everyday needs of the masses of the workers and of the toilers generally, in utilizing the bourgeois parliament as a platform for revolutionary agitation and propaganda, and subordinating the partial tasks to the struggle for the dictatorship of the proletariat, the Parties of the Communist International advance partial demands and slogans in the following main spheres:

In the sphere of *labor,* in the narrow meaning of the term, *i.e.,* questions concerned with the *economic* struggle (the fight against the offensive of trustified capital, wage questions, the working day, compulsory arbitration, unemployment), which grow into questions of the general political struggle (big industrial conflicts, fight for the right to organize, right to strike, etc.); in the sphere of *politics* proper (taxation, high cost of living, Fascism, persecution of revolutionary parties, white terror and current politics generally); and finally the sphere of *world* politics, *viz.,* attitude towards the U.S.S.R. and colonial revolutions, struggle for the unity of the international trade union movement, struggle against imperialism and the war danger, and systematic preparation for the fight against *imperialist war.*

In the sphere of the *peasant* problem, the partial demands are those appertaining to taxation, peasant mortgage indebtedness, struggle against usurer's capital, the land hunger of the peasant smallholders, rent, the metayer (crop-sharing) system. Starting out from these partial needs, the Communist Party must sharpen the respective slogans broadening them out into the slogans: confiscation of large estates, and workers' and peasants' government (the synonym for proletarian dictatorship in developed capitalist countries and of democratic dictatorship of the proletariat and peasantry for backward countries and in certain colonies).

Systematic work must also be carried on among the proletarian and peasant *youth* (mainly through the Young Communist International and its Sections) and also among the *working women and peasant women.* This work must concern itself with the special conditions of life and struggle of the working and peasant women, and their demands must be linked up with the general demands and fighting slogans of the proletariat.

In the struggle against *colonial oppression,* the Communist Parties in the colonies must advance partial demands that correspond to the special circumstances prevailing in each country such as: complete equality for all nations and races; abolition of all privileges for foreigners; the right of association for workers and peasants; reduction of the working day; prohibition of child labor; prohibition of usury and of all transactions entailing bondage; reduction and abolition of rent; reduction of taxation; refusal to pay taxes, etc. All these partial slogans must be subordinated to the fundamental demands of the Communist Parties such as: complete political national independence and the expulsion of the imperialists; workers' and peasants' government, the land to the whole people, eight-hour day, etc. The Communist Parties in *imperialist countries,* while supporting the struggle proceeding in the colonies, must carry on a campaign in their own respective countries for the withdrawal of imperialist troops, conduct propaganda in the army and navy in defense of the oppressed countries fighting for their liberation, mobilize the masses to refuse to transport troops and munitions, and in connection with this, organize strikes and other forms of mass protest, etc.

Programme of the Communist International, Chapter VI, part 2, pp. 57-63.

3. The Fight for the United Proletarian Front Against Fascism at the Present Stage

A. The United Front of the Working Class Against Fascism

In face of the towering menace of fascism to the working class and all the gains it has made, to all toilers and their elementary rights, to the peace and liberty of the peoples, the Seventh Congress of the Communist International declares that *at the present historic stage it is the main and immediate task of the international labor movement to establish the united fighting front of the working class.* For a successful struggle against the offensive of capital, against the reactionary measures of the bourgeoisie, against fascism, the bitterest enemy of all the toilers, who, without distinction of political views, have been deprived of all rights and liberties, it is imperative that unity of action be established between all sections of the working class, irrespective of what organization they belong to, even before the majority of the working class unites on a common fighting platform for the overthrow of capitalism and the victory of the proletarian revolution. But it is precisely for this very reason that this task makes it the duty of the Communist Parties to take into consideration the changed circumstances and to apply the united front tactics *in a new manner,* by seeking to reach agreements with the organizations of the toilers of various political trends for joint action on a factory, local, district, national and international scale.

With this as its point of departure, the Seventh Congress of the Communist International enjoins the Communist Parties to be guided by the following instructions when carrying out the united front tactics:

1. *The defence of the immediate economic and political interests of the working class, the defense of the latter against fascism,* must be the starting point and form the main content of the workers' united front in all capitalist countries. In order to set the broad masses in motion, such slogans and forms of struggle must be put forward as arise from the vital needs of the masses and from the level of their fighting capacity at the given stage of development. Communists must not limit themselves merely to issuing appeals to struggle for proletarian dictatorship, but must show the masses *what they are to do today* to defend themselves against capitalist plunder and fascist barbarity. They must strive, through the joint action of the labor organizations, to mobilize the masses around *a program of demands that are calculated really to shift the burden of the consequences of the crisis to the shoulders of the ruling classes – of demands, the fight for whose realization will disorganize fascism, hamper the preparations for imperialist war, weaken the bourgeoisie and strengthen the positions of the proletariat.*

While preparing the working class for rapid shifts in the forms and methods of struggle as circumstances change, it is necessary to organize, in proportion as the movement grows, the transition *from the defensive to the offensive* against capital, steering toward the organization of a *mass political strike,* in which it is indispensable that the participation of the principal trade unions of the country should be secured.

2. Without for a moment giving up their independent work in

the sphere of Communist education, organization and mobilization of the masses, the Communists, in order to render the road to unity of action easier for the workers, must *strive to secure joint action with the Social-Democratic Parties, reformist trade unions and other organizations of the toilers against the class enemies of the proletariat, on the basis of short or long-term agreements.* At the same time, attention must be directed mainly to the development of mass action in the various localities, conducted by the *lower organizations* through local agreements.

Loyally fulfilling the conditions of the agreements, the Communists must promptly expose any sabotage of joint action by persons or organizations participating in the united front, and if the agreement is broken, must immediately appeal to the masses while continuing their tireless struggle for the restoration of the disrupted unity of action.

3. The forms in which the united proletarian front is realized, which depend on the condition and character of the labor organizations and on the concrete situation, must be varied in character. Such forms may include, for instance, agreed-upon joint action by the workers *from case to case, on particular* occasions, to secure individual demands, or on the basis of a common platform; action agreed upon in *individual enterprises or branches of industry;* action agreed upon on a *local, district, national or international scale;* action agreed upon in the organization of the *economic struggle* of the workers, in defense of the interests of the unemployed, in carrying out mass *political* activity, in the organization of joint *self-defense* against fascist attacks; action agreed upon to render *aid to political prisoners and their families,* in the field of struggle against *social* reaction; joint action in defense of the *interests of the youth and women,* in the sphere of the *cooperative movement, cultural activity and sports;* joint action for the purpose of supporting the demands of the toiling peasants, etc.; the formation of workers', and workers' and peasants' alliances (Spain); the formation of lasting coalitions in the shape of "Labor Parties" or "Farmer Labor Parties" (U.S.A.), etc.

In order to develop the united front movement as the cause of the masses themselves, Communists must strive to secure the establishment of elective (or, in the countries under fascist dictatorship, selected from the most authoritative participants in the movement) *non-party class organs of the united front* in the factories, among the unemployed, in the working class districts, among the petty townsfolk, and in the villages. Only such bodies (which, of course, should not supplant the organizations participating in the united front) will be able to bring into the united front movement also the vast *unorganized mass* of toilers, will be able to assist in developing the initiative of the masses in the struggle against the offensive of capital and against fascism, and on this basis help to create a large body of working class united front activists.

4. Wherever the Social-Democratic leaders, in their efforts to deflect the workers from the struggle in defense of their everyday interests and in order to frustrate the united front, put forward *widely advertised "Socialist"* projects (the de Man plan, etc.), the demagogic nature of such projects must be exposed, and the toilers must be shown the impossibility of bringing about Socialism so long as power remains in the hands of the bourgeoisie. At the same time, however, some of the measures put forward in these projects that can be linked up with the vital demands of the toilers should be utilized as *the starting point for developing a mass united front struggle jointly with the Social-Democratic workers.*

In countries where *Social-Democratic governments* are in power (or where there are coalition governments in which Socialists participate), Communists must not confine themselves to propaganda exposing the policies of such governments, but must mobilize the broad masses for the struggle to secure their practical vital class demands, the fulfillment of which the Social-Democrats announced in their platforms, particularly when they were not yet in power or were not yet members of their respective governments.

5. Joint action with the Social-Democratic Parties and organizations not only does not preclude, but, on the contrary, *renders still more necessary* the serious and well-founded criticism of reformism, of Social-Democracy as the ideology and practice of class collaboration with the bourgeoisie, and the patient exposition of the principles and program of Communism to the Social-Democratic workers.

While revealing to the masses the meaning of the demagogic arguments advanced by the Right Social-Democratic leaders against the united front, *while intensifying the struggle against the reactionary section of* Social-Democracy, the Communists must establish *the closest cooperation with those Left Social-Democratic workers, functionaries and organizations that fight against the reformist policy and advocate a united front with the Communist Party.* The more we intensify our fight against the reactionary camp of Social-Democracy, which is participating in a bloc with the bourgeoisie, the more effective will be the assistance we give to that part of Social-Democracy which is becoming revolutionized. And the self-determination of the various elements within the Left camp will take place the sooner, the more resolutely the Communists fight for a united front with the Social-Democratic Parties.

The attitude to the practical realization of the united front will be the chief indication of the true position of the various groups among the Social-Democrats. In the fight for the practical realization of the united front, those Social-Democratic leaders who came forward as Lefts in words will be obliged to show by deeds whether they are really ready to fight the bourgeoisie and the Right Social-Democrats, or are on the side of the bourgeoisie, that is, against the cause of the working class.

6. *Election campaigns* must be utilized for the further development and strengthening of the united fighting front of the proletariat. While coming forward independently in the elections and unfolding the program of the Communist Party before the masses, the Communists must seek to establish a united front with the Social-Democratic Parties and the trade unions (also with the organizations of the toiling peasants, handicraftsmen, etc.), and exert every effort to prevent the election of reactionary and fascist candidates. In face of fascist danger, the Communists, *while reserving for themselves freedom of political agitation and criticism*, may, in election campaigns, *declare for a common platform and a common ticket with the anti-fascist front*, depending on the growth and success of the united front movement, and on the electoral system in operation.

7. In striving to unite, under the leadership of the proletariat, the struggle of the toiling peasants, the urban petty bourgeoisie and the toiling masses of the oppressed nationalities, the Communists must seek to bring about the establishment of a wide *anti-fascist people's front* on the basis of the proletarian united front, supporting all those specific demands of these sections of the toilers which are in line with the fundamental interests of the proletariat. It is particularly important to mobilize the *toiling peasants* against the fascist policy of robbing the basic masses of the peasantry; against the plundering price policy of monopoly capital and the bourgeois gov-

ernments, against the unbearable burden of taxes, rents and debts, against forced sales of peasant property, and in favor of government aid for the ruined peasantry. While working everywhere among the *urban petty bourgeoisie and the intelligentsia* as well as among the *office workers,* the Communists must rouse these sections against increasing taxation and the high cost of living, against their spoliation by monopoly capital, by the trusts, against the thraldom of interest payments, and against dismissals and reductions in salary of government and municipal employees. While defending the interests and rights of the progressive intellectuals, it is necessary to give them every support in their movement against cultural reaction, and to facilitate their going over to the side of the working class in the struggle against fascism.

8. In the circumstances of a political crisis, when the ruling classes are no longer in a position to cope with the powerful sweep of the mass movement, the Communists must advance *fundamental* revolutionary slogans (such as, for instance, control of production and the banks, disbandments of the police force and its replacement by an armed workers' militia, etc.), which are directed toward still further shaking the economic and political power of the bourgeoisie and increasing the strength of the working class, toward isolating the parties of compromise, and which lead the working masses right up to the point of the revolutionary seizure of power. If with such an upsurge of the mass movement it will prove possible, and necessary in the interests of the proletariat, to create a *proletarian united front government,* or an *anti-fascist people's front government,* which is not yet a government of the proletarian dictatorship, but one which undertakes to put into effect decisive measures against fascism and reaction, the Communist Party must see to it that such a government is formed. The following situation is an essential prerequisite for the formation of a united front government: (a) when the state apparatus of the bourgeoisie is seriously paralyzed so that the bourgeoisie is not in a condition to prevent the formation of such a government; (b) when vast masses of the toilers vehemently take action against fascism and reaction, but are not yet ready to rise and fight for Soviet power; (c) when already a considerable proportion of the organizations of the Social-Democratic and other parties participating in the united front demand ruthless measures against the fascists and other reactionaries, and are ready to fight together with the Communists for the carrying out of these measures.

In so far as the united front government will really undertake decisive measures against the counter-revolutionary financial magnates and their fascist agents, and will in no way restrict the activity of the Communist Party and the struggle of the working class, the Communist Party will support such a government in every way. The participation of the Communists in a united front government will be decided separately in each particular case, as the concrete situation may warrant.

B. The Unity of the Trade Union Movement

Emphasizing the special importance of forming a united front in the sphere of the economic struggle of the workers and the establishment of the unity of the trade union movement as a most important step in consolidating the united front of the proletariat, the Congress makes it a duty of the Communists to adopt all practical measures for the realization of the unity of the trade unions by industries and on a national scale.

The Communists are decidedly for the reestablishment of trade union unity in each country and on an international scale; for united class trade unions as one of the major bulwarks of the working class against the offensive of capital and fascism; for one trade union in each industry; for one trade union center in each country; for one international federation of trade unions organized according to the industries; for one international of trade unions based on the class struggle.

In countries where small Red trade unions exist, efforts must be made to secure their admission to the big reformist trade unions, with demands put forward for the right to defend their views and the reinstatement of expelled members. In countries where big Red and reformist trade unions exist side by side, efforts must be made to secure their amalgamation on an equal footing, on the basis of a platform of struggle against the offensive of capital and a guarantee of trade union democracy.

It is the duty of Communists to work actively in the reformist and united trade unions, to consolidate them and to recruit the unorganized workers for them, and at the same time exert every effort to have these organizations actually defend the interests of the workers and really become genuine class organizations. To this end the Communists must strive to secure the support of the entire membership, of the officials, and of the organizations as a whole.

It is the duty of Communists to defend the trade unions against all attempts on the part of the bourgeoisie and fascism to restrict their rights or to destroy them.

If the reformist leaders resort to the policy of expelling revolutionary workers or entire branches of unions, or adopt other forms of repression, the Communists must rally the entire union membership against the splitting activity of the leadership, at the same time establishing contact between the expelled members and the bulk of the members of the trade unions, and engaging in a joint struggle for their reinstatement, for the restoration of the disrupted trade union unity.

The Red trade unions and the Red International of Labor Unions must receive the fullest support of the Communist Parties in their efforts to bring about the joint struggle of the trade unions of all trends, and establish unity in the trade union movement both nationally and internationally, *on the basis of the class struggle and trade union democracy.*

C. Tasks of the Communists in the Individual Sectors of the Anti-Fascist Movement

1. The Congress calls particular attention to the necessity of carrying on a systematic *ideological struggle against fascism.* In view of the fact that the chief, the most dangerous form of fascist ideology is *chauvinism,* it must be made plain to the masses that the fascist bourgeoisie uses the pretext of defending the national interests to carry out its sordid class policy of oppressing and exploiting its own people as well as robbing and enslaving other peoples. They must be shown that the working class, which fights against every form of servitude and national oppression, is *the only genuine protagonist of national freedom and the independence of the people.* The Communists must in every way combat the fascist falsification of the history of the people, and do everything to enlighten the toiling masses on the past of their own people in an historically correct fashion, in the true spirit of Lenin and Stalin, so as to link up their present struggle with the revolutionary traditions of the past. The Congress warns against adopting a disparaging attitude on the question of national independence and the national sentiments of the broad masses of the people, an attitude which renders it easier for fascism to develop its chauvinist campaigns (the Saar, the German regions in Czechoslovakia, etc.), and insists on a correct and con-

crete application of the Leninist-Stalinist national policy.

While Communists are irreconcilable opponents, on principle, of bourgeois nationalism of every variety, they are by no means supporters of national nihilism, of an attitude of unconcern for the fate of their own people.

2. Communists must enter all *fascist mass* organizations which have a monopoly of legal existence in the given country, and must make use of even the smallest legal or semi-legal opportunity of working in them, in order to counterpose the interests of the masses in these organizations to the policy of fascism, and to undermine the mass basis of the latter. Beginning with the most elementary movements of protest around the urgent needs of the toilers, the Communists must use flexible tactics to draw ever wider masses into the movement, especially workers who by reason of their lack of class consciousness still follow the fascists. As the movement gains in width and depth, the slogans of the struggle must be changed, while preparing to smash the fascist bourgeois dictatorship with the aid of the very masses that are in the fascist organizations.

3. While vigorously and consistently defending the interests and demands of the unemployed, while organizing and leading them in the fight for work, for adequate relief, insurance, etc., the Communists must draw the unemployed into the united front movement and use all means to force out the influence of fascism among them. At the same time it is necessary to take strictly into account the specific interests of the various categories of unemployed (skilled and unskilled workers, organized and unorganized, men and women, youth, etc.).

4. The Congress emphatically calls the attention of all Communist Parties of the capitalist countries to the exceptional role of the youth in the struggle against fascism. It is from among the youth that fascism mainly recruits its shock detachments. In fighting against any underestimation of the importance of *mass work among the toiling youth,* and taking effective steps to overcome the secludedness of the Young Communist League organizations, the Communist Parties must do everything to help unite the forces of all non-fascist mass youth organizations, including youth organizations of the trade unions, cooperative societies, etc., on the basis of the broadest united front, including the formation of various kinds of common organizations for the struggle against fascism, against the unprecedented manner in which the youth is being stripped of

every right, against the militarization of the youth, and for the economic and cultural interests of the young generation. The task of creating an anti-fascist association of Communist and Socialist youth leagues on the platform of the class struggle must be brought to the fore.

The Communist Parties must give every assistance in the development and consolidation of the Young Communist Leagues.

5. The vital necessity of drawing the millions of toiling *women* into the united people's front, primarily women workers and toiling peasant women, irrespective of the political and religious views they hold, requires that the Communists intensify their activity for the purpose of developing the mass movement of the toiling women around the struggle for their urgent demands and interests, particularly in the struggle against the high cost of living, against inequality in the status of women and their fascist enslavement, against mass dismissals, for higher wages on the principle of "equal pay for equal work," and against the war danger. Flexible use must be made, in every country and on an international scale, of the most varied organizational forms to establish contacts between and bring about joint action of the revolutionary, Social-Democratic and progressive women's organizations, while ensuring freedom of opinion and criticism, without hesitating to form also separate women's organizations wherever this may become necessary.

6. Communists must carry on a struggle to draw the co-operative organizations into the ranks of the united front of the proletariat and of the anti-fascist people's front....

D. For Soviet Power!

In the struggle to defend against fascism the bourgeois-democratic liberties and the gains of the toilers, in the struggle to overthrow fascist dictatorship, the revolutionary proletariat prepares its forces, strengthens its fighting contacts with its allies and directs the struggle toward the goal of achieving real democracy of the toilers – Soviet power.

The further consolidation of the Land of the Soviets, the rallying of the world proletariat around it, and the mighty growth of the international authority of the Communist Party of the Soviet Union, the turn toward revolutionary class struggle which has set in among the Social-Democratic workers and the workers organized in the reformist trade unions, the increasing mass resistance to fascism and the growth of the revolutionary movement in the colonies, the decline of the Second International and the growth of the Communist International, *are all accelerating and will continue to accelerate the development of the world Socialist revolution.*

The capitalist world is entering a period of sharp clashes as a result of the accentuation of the internal and external contradictions of capitalism.

Steering a course in the direction of this perspective of the revolutionary development, the Seventh Congress of the Communist International calls on the Communist Parties to display the greatest political activity and daring, to carry on a tireless struggle to bring about unity of action by the working class. *The establishment of the united front of the working class is the decisive link in the preparation of the toilers for the forthcoming great battles of the second round of proletarian revolutions.* Only the welding of the proletariat into a single mass political army will ensure its victory in the struggle against fascism and the power of capital, for the dictatorship of the proletariat and the power of the Soviets. *"The victory of revolution never comes by itself. It has to be prepared for* and won. And only a strong proletarian revolutionary party can prepare for and win victory." *(Stalin.)*

Seventh World Congress of the Communist International, Resolution, on the Report of Georgi Dimitrov, pp. 17-28; 33-34.

4. The Anti-Fascist People's Front

In the mobilization of the toiling masses for the struggle against fascism, the formation of a *broad people's anti-fascist front* on the *basis of the proletarian united front* is a particularly important task. The success of the entire struggle of the proletariat is closely connected with the establishment of a fighting alliance between the proletariat on the one hand and the toiling peasantry and the basic mass of the urban petty bourgeoisie constituting a majority in the population of even industrially developed countries, on the other.

In its agitation, fascism, desirous of winning these masses to its own side, tries to set the toiling masses of the cities and the countryside against the revolutionary proletariat, intimidating the petty bourgeoisie with the bugaboo of the "Red danger." We must *turn the spearpoint in the opposite direction* and show the toiling peasants, artisans and toiling intellectuals whence the real danger threatens. We must *show* them *concretely* who piles the burden of taxes and imposts on to the peasant, squeezes usurious interest out of him, and who, while owning the best lands and enjoying every form of wealth, drives the peasant and his family from his plot of land and dooms him to unemployment and poverty. We must explain concretely, explain patiently and persistently, who ruins the artisans, the handicraftsmen, with taxes, imposts, high rents and competition impossible for them to withstand, who throws into the street and deprives of employment the broad masses of the toiling intelligentsia.

But this is *not enough.*

The fundamental, the most decisive point in establishing the anti-fascist people's front is *the resolute action of the revolutionary proletariat* in defense of the demands of these sections particularly of the toiling peasantry, demands in line with the basic interests of the proletariat, combining in the process of struggle the demands of the working class with these demands.

In forming the anti-fascist people's front, a correct approach to those organizations and parties to which a considerable number of the toiling peasantry and the mass of the urban petty bourgeoisie belong is of great importance.

In the capitalist countries the majority of these parties and organizations, political as well as economic, are still under the influence of the bourgeoisie and follow it. The social composition of these parties and organizations is heterogeneous. They include big kulaks (rich peasants) side by side with landless peasants, big business men alongside of petty shopkeepers, but control is in the hands of the former, the agents of big capital. This makes it our duty to *approach* these organizations in *different ways,* taking into consideration that not infrequently the bulk of the membership does not know anything about the real political character of its leadership. Under certain conditions, we can and must bend our efforts to the task of drawing these parties and organizations or certain sections of them to the side of the ant-fascist people's front, despite their bourgeois leadership. Such, for instance, is today the situation in France with the Radical Party, in the United States with various farmers' organizations, in Poland with the "Stronnictwo Ludowe," in Jugoslavia with the Croatian Peasants' Party, in Bulgaria with the Agrarian League, in Greece with the Agrarians, etc. But irrespective of whether there is any chance of attracting these parties and organizations to the side of the people's front, our tactics must *under all circumstances* be directed toward drawing the small peasants, artisans, handicraftsmen, etc., among their members into the anti-fascist people's front.

You see consequently that in this field we must put an end all along the line to what frequently occurs in our practical work – the ignoring of or contemptuous attitude toward the various organizations and parties of the peasants, artisans and urban petty-bourgeois masses.

5. Cardinal Questions of the United Front in Individual Countries

There are in every country certain *cardinal questions* which at the present stage are agitating vast masses of the population and around which the struggle for the establishment of the united front must be developed. If these cardinal points, cardinal questions, are properly grasped, it will ensure and accelerate the establishment of the united front.

(a) *The United States of America*

Let us take, for example, so important a country in the capitalist world as the *United States of America.* Three millions of people have been brought into motion by the crisis. The program for the recovery of capitalism has collapsed. Vast masses are beginning to abandon the bourgeois parties, and are at present at the crossroads.

Incipient American fascism is endeavoring to direct the disillusionment and discontent of these masses into reactionary fascist channels. It is a peculiarity of the development of American fascism that at the present stage it appears principally in the guise of an opposition to fascism, which it accuses of being an "un-American" tendency imported from abroad. In contradistinction to German fascism, which acts under anti-constitutional slogans, American fascism tries to portray itself as the custodian of the constitution and "American democracy." It does not yet represent a directly menacing force. But if it succeeds in penetrating to the broad masses who have become disillusioned with the old bourgeois parties, it may become a serious menace in the very near future.

And what would the success of fascism in the United States entail? For the toiling masses it would, of course, entail the unrestrained strengthening of the regime of exploitation and the destruction of the working class movement. And what would be the international significance of this success of fascism? As we know, the United States is not Hungary, or Finland, or Bulgaria, or Latvia. The success of fascism in the United States would change the whole international situation quite materially.

Under these circumstances, can the American proletariat content itself with the organization of only its class conscious vanguard, which is prepared to follow the revolutionary path? No.

It is perfectly obvious that the interests of the American proletariat demand that all its forces dissociate themselves from the capitalist parties without delay. It must at the proper time find ways and suitable forms of preventing fascism from winning over the broad and discontented masses of the toilers. And here it must be said that under American conditions the creation of a mass party of toilers, a *Farmer-Labor Party*, might serve as such a suitable form. *Such a party would be a specific form of the mass people's front in America* that should be set up in opposition to the parties of the trusts and the banks, and likewise to growing fascism. Such a party, of course, will be *neither* Socialist *nor* Communist. But it *must be* an anti-fascist party and *must not be* an anti-Communist party. The program of this party must be directed against the banks, trusts and monopolies, against the principal enemies of the people who are gambling on its misfortunes. Such a party will be equal to its task only if it defends the urgent demands of the working class, only if it fights for genuine social legislation, for unemployment insurance; only if it fights for land for the white and black share-croppers and for their liberation from the burden of debt; only if it works for the cancellation of the farmers' indebtedness; only if it fights for the equal status of the Negroes; only if it fights for the demands of the ex-servicemen, and for the interests of the members of the liberal professions, the small business men, the artisans. And so on.

It goes without saying that such a party will fight for the election of its own candidates to local offices, to the state legislatures, to the House of Representatives and the Senate.

Our comrades in the United States acted rightly in taking the initiative for the creation of such a party. But they still have to take effective measures in order to make the creation of such a party the cause of the masses themselves. The question of forming a Farmer-Labor Party, and its program, should be discussed at mass meetings of the people. We should develop the most widespread movement for the creation of such a party, and take the lead in it. In no case must the initiative of organizing the party be allowed to pass to elements desirous of utilizing the discontent of the masses which have become disillusioned in both the bourgeois parties, Democratic and Republican, in order to create a "third party" in the United States, as an anti-Communist party, a party directed against the revolutionary movement.

(b) *Great Britain*

In *Great Britain,* as a result of the mass action of the British workers, Mosley's fascist organization has for the time being been pushed into the background. But we must not close our eyes to the fact that the so-called "National Government" is passing a number of reactionary measures directed against the working class, as a result of which conditions are being created in Great Britain, too, which will make it easy for the bourgeoisie, if necessary, to proceed to a fascist regime. At the present stage, fighting the fascist danger in Great Britain means primarily fighting the "National Government" and its reactionary measures, fighting the offensive of capital, fighting for the demands of the unemployed, fighting against wage reductions and for the repeal of all those laws with the help of which the British bourgeoisie is lowering the standard of living of the masses.

But the growing hatred of the working class for the "National Government" .is uniting increasingly large numbers under the slogan of the formation of a *new Labor Government* in Great Britain. Can the Communists ignore this frame of mind of the masses, who still retain faith in a Labor Government? No. We must find a way of approaching these masses. We tell them openly, as did the Thirteenth Congress of the British Communist Party, that we Communists are in favor of a Soviet government, as the only form of government capable of emancipating the workers from the yoke of capital. But you want a Labor Government? Very well. We have been and are fighting hand in hand with you for the defeat of the "National Government." We are prepared to support your fight for the formation of a new Labor Government, in spite of the fact that both the previous Labor Governments did not fulfill the promises made to the working class by the Labor Party. We do not expect this government to carry out Socialist measures. But *we shall present it with the demand,* in the name of the working class millions, that it defend the most essential economic and political interests of the working class and of all the toilers. Let us jointly discuss a common program of such demands, and let us achieve that unity of action which the proletariat requires in order to repel the reactionary offensive of the "National Government," the attack of capital and fascism, and the preparations for a new war. On this basis, the British comrades are prepared at the forthcoming parliamentary elections to cooperate with branches of the Labor Party against the "National Government," and also against Lloyd George, who is endeavoring in his own way to lure the masses into following him against the cause of the working class and in the interests of the British bourgeoisie.

This position of the British Communists is a correct one. It will help them to set up a militant united front with the millions of members of the British trade unions and the British Labor Party.

While always remaining in the front ranks of the fighting proletariat, and pointing out to the masses the only right path – the path of struggle for the revolutionary overthrow of the rule of the bourgeoisie and the establishment of a Soviet government – the Communists, in defining their immediate political aims, must not attempt to leap over those necessary stages of the mass movement in the course of which the working class masses by their own experience outlive their illusions and pass over to the side of Communism.

(c) *France*

France, as we know, is a country in which the working class is setting an example to the whole world proletariat of how to fight fascism. The French Communist Party is setting an example to all the sections of the Comintern of how the tactics of the united front should be conducted; the Socialist workers are setting an example of what the Social-Democratic workers of other capitalist countries should now be doing in the fight against fascism. The significance of the anti-fascist demonstration, attended by half a million people, held in Paris on July 14 of this year[*] and of the numerous demonstrations in other French cities is tremendous. This is not merely a movement of a united working class front; it is the beginning of a wide general front of the people against fascism in France.

This united front movement enhances the confidence of the working class in its own forces; it strengthens its consciousness of

---

[*] 1935. – *Ed.*

the leading role it is playing in relation to the peasantry, the petty bourgeoisie of the towns and the intelligentsia; it extends the influence of the Communist Party among the working class masses, and therefore brings new strength to the proletariat in the fight against fascism. It is mobilizing in good time the vigilance of the masses in regard to the fascist danger. And it will serve as an infectious example for the development of the anti-fascist struggle in other capitalist countries and will exercise a heartening influence on the proletarians of Germany, crushed down by the fascist dictatorship.

The victory, needless to say, is a big one, but it still does not decide the issue of the anti-fascist struggle. The overwhelming majority of the French people are undoubtedly opposed to fascism. But the bourgeoisie is able by armed force to violate the will of peoples. The fascist movement is continuing to develop absolutely freely, with the active support of monopoly capital, the state apparatus of the bourgeoisie, the general staff of the French army, and the reactionary leaders of the Catholic church – that stronghold of all reaction. The most powerful fascist organization, the *Croix de Feu,* now commands 300,000 armed men, the backbone of which consists of 60,000 officers of the reserve. It holds strong positions in the police, the gendarmerie, the army, the air force and in all government offices. The recent municipal elections have shown that in France it is not only the revolutionary forces that are growing, but also the forces of fascism. If fascism succeeds in penetrating widely among the peasantry, and in securing the support of one section of the army, while the other section remains neutral, the French toiling masses will not be able to prevent the fascists from coming to power. Do not forget the organizational weakness of the French labor movement, which tends to facilitate the success of the fascist attack. The working class and all anti-fascists in France have no ground for resting content with the results already achieved.

What are the tasks confronting the working class in France?

First, to achieve the establishment of a united front not only in the political sphere, but also in the economic sphere in order to organize the struggle against the capitalist offensive, and by its pressure to smash the resistance offered to the united front by the leaders of the reformist Confederation of Labor.

Second, to achieve trade union unity in France – united trade unions based on the class struggle.

Third, to enlist in the anti-fascist movement the broad peasant masses, the petty-bourgeois masses, devoting special attention in the program of the anti-fascist people's front to their urgent demands.

Fourth, to strengthen organizationally and extend further the anti-fascist movement which has already developed, by the widespread creation of elected non-party bodies of the anti-fascist people's front, the influence of which extends to wider masses than those in the parties and the organizations of the toilers in France at present in existence.

Fifth, to secure by their pressure the disbanding and disarming of the fascist organizations, as organizations of conspirators against the Republic and agents of Hitler in France.

Sixth, to achieve the purging of the state apparatus, the army and the police of the conspirators who are preparing a fascist coup.

Seventh, to develop the struggle against the leaders of the reactionary cliques of the Catholic church, as one of the most important strongholds of French fascism.

Eighth, to link up the army with the anti-fascist movement by creating in its ranks committees for the defense of the Republic and the constitution, directed against those who want to utilize the army for an anti-constitutional *coup d'état;* not to allow the reactionary forces in France to wreck the Franco-Soviet pact, which defends the cause of peace against the aggression of German fascism.

And if in France the anti-fascist movement leads to the formation of a government which will carry on a real struggle against French fascism – not in word but in deed – will carry out the program of demands of the anti-fascist people's front, the Communists, *while remaining* the irreconcilable foes of every bourgeois government, and while remaining supporters of a Soviet government, will nevertheless, in face of the growing fascist danger, *be prepared to support such a government.*

6. The Tactics of the Communist International in Connection with the Preparation of a New World War by the Imperialists

A. The Struggle for Peace and Against Imperialist War

On the basis of the teaching of Marx, Engels, Lenin, and Stalin on war, the Sixth World Congress of the Communist International concretely formulated the tasks of the Communist Parties and the revolutionary proletariat in the struggle against imperialist war. Guided by these principles, the Communist Parties of Japan and

China, both directly affected by war, have waged and are waging a Bolshevik struggle against imperialist war and for the defense of the Chinese people. *The Seventh World Congress of the Communist International, confirming the decisions of the Sixth Congress on the struggle against imperialist war,* sets the following main tasks before the Communist Parties, the revolutionary workers, toilers, peasants and oppressed peoples of the whole world:

1. *The struggle for peace and for the defense of the U.S.S.R.* In face of the war provocations of the German fascists and Japanese militarists, and the speeding up of armaments by the war parties in the capitalist countries, in face of the immediate danger of a counter-revolutionary war breaking out against the Soviet Union, the *central slogan* of the Communist Parties must be: struggle for peace.

2. *The United People's Front in the struggle for peace and against the instigators of war.* The struggle for peace opens up before the Communist Parties the greatest opportunities for creating the broadest united front. All those interested in the preservation of peace should be drawn into this united front. The concentration of forces against the chief instigators of war at any given moment (at the present time – against fascist Germany, and against Poland and Japan which are in league with it) constitutes a most important tactical task of the Communist Parties. It is of especially great importance for the Communist Party of Germany to expose the national demagogy of Hitler fascism, which screens itself behind phrases about the unification of the German people but in fact leads to the isolation of the German people and to a new war catastrophe. The overthrow of Hitler fascism is an indispensable condition and prerequisite for the unification of the German people. The establishment of a united front with Social-Democratic and reformist organizations (party, trade union, cooperative, sports, and cultural and educational organizations) and with the bulk of their members, also with mass national-liberation, religious-democratic and pacifist organizations and their adherents, is of decisive importance for the struggle against war and its fascist instigators in all countries.

The formation of a united front with *Social-Democratic and reformist* organizations for the struggle for peace necessitates a determined ideological struggle against the reactionary elements within the Social-Democratic Parties which, in face of the immediate danger of war, proceed to collaborate even more closely with the bourgeoisie for the defense of the bourgeois fatherland, and by their campaigns of slander against the Soviet Union directly aid the preparations for an anti-Soviet war. It necessitates close collaboration with those forces in the Social-Democratic Parties, reformist trade unions and other mass labor organizations whose position is approaching ever closer to that of revolutionary struggle against imperialist war.

The drawing of pacifist organizations and their adherents into the united front of struggle for peace acquires great importance in mobilizing the petty-bourgeois masses, progressive intellectuals, women and youth against war. While constantly subjecting the erroneous views of sincere pacifists to constructive criticism, and vigorously combating those pacifists who by their policy screen the preparations of the German fascists for imperialist war (the leadership of the Labor Party in Great Britain, etc.), the Communists must invite the collaboration of all pacifist organizations that are prepared to go with them even if only part of the way towards a genuine struggle against imperialist wars.

The Communists must support the Amsterdam-Pleyel anti-war and anti-fascist movement by active collaboration with it and help to extend it.

3. *The combination of the struggle against imperialist war with the struggle against fascism.* The anti-war struggle of the masses striving to preserve peace must be very closely combined with the struggle against fascism and the fascist movement. It is necessary to conduct not only general propaganda for peace, but primarily propaganda directed against the chief instigators of war, against the fascist and other imperialist war parties, and against concrete measures of preparation for imperialist war.

4. *The struggle against militarism and armaments.* The Communist Parties of all capitalist countries must fight: Against military expenditures (war budgets), for the recall of military forces from the colonies and mandated territories, against militarization measures taken by capitalist governments, especially the militarization of the youth, women and the unemployed, against emergency decrees restricting bourgeois-democratic liberties with the aim of preparing for war; against restricting the rights of workers employed in war industry plants, against subsidizing the war industry and against trading in or transporting arms. The struggle against war preparation measures can be conducted only in closest connec-

tion with the defense of the economic interests and political rights of the workers, office employees, toiling peasants and urban petty bourgeoisie.

5. *The struggle against chauvinism.* In the struggle against chauvinism the task of the Communists consists in educating the workers and the whole of the toiling population in the spirit of pro-letarian internationalism, which can be accomplished only in the struggle against the exploiters and oppressors for the vital class in-terests of the proletariat, as well as in the struggle against the bestial chauvinism of the National-Socialist Parties and all other fascist parties. At the same time the Communists must show that the work-ing class carries on a consistent struggle in defense of the national freedom and independence of all the people against any oppression or exploitation, because only the Communist policy defends to the very end the national freedom and independence of the people of one's country.

6. *The national liberation struggle and the support of wars of national liberation.* If any weak state is attacked by one or more big imperialist powers which want to destroy its national independence and national unity or to dismember it, as in the historic instance of the partition of Poland, a war conducted by the national bourgeoisie of such a country to repel this attack may assume the character of a war of liberation, in which the working class and the Communists of that country cannot abstain from intervening. It is the task of the Communists of such a country, while carrying on an irreconcilable struggle to safeguard the economic and political positions of the workers, toiling peasants and national minorities, to be, at the same time, in the front ranks of the fighters for national independence and to fight the war of liberation to a finish, without allowing "their" bourgeoisie to strike a bargain with the attacking powers to the prejudice of the interests of their country.

It is the duty of the Communists actively to support the nation-al liberation struggle of the oppressed peoples of the colonial and semi-colonial countries, especially the Red Army of the Chinese Soviets, in their struggle against the Japanese and other imperialists and the Kuomintang. The Communist Party of China must exert every effort to extend the front of the struggle for national libera-tion and to draw into it all the national forces that are ready to re-pulse the robber campaign of the Japanese and other imperialists.

B. From the Struggle for Peace to the Struggle for Revolution

The Seventh World Congress of the Communist International most determinedly repudiates the slanderous contention that Communists desire war, expecting it to bring revolution. The leading role of the Communist Parties of all countries in the struggle for the preservation of peace, for the triumph of the peace policy of the Soviet Union, proves that the Communists are striving with all their might to obstruct the preparations for and the unleashing of a new war.

The Communists, while fighting also against the illusion that war can be eliminated while the capitalist system still exists, are exerting and will exert every effort to prevent war. Should a new imperialist world war break out, despite all efforts of the working class to prevent it, the Communists will strive to lead the opponents of war, organized in the struggle for peace, to the struggle for the transformation of the imperialist war into civil war against the fascist instigators of war, against the bourgeoisie, for the overthrow of capitalism.

The Congress at the same time warns the Communists and revolutionary workers against anarcho-syndicalist methods of struggle against war, which take the form of refusing to appear for military service, the form of a so-called boycott of mobilization, of committing sabotage in war plants, etc. The Congress considers that such methods of struggle only do harm to the proletariat. The Russian Bolsheviks who, during the World War, fought energetically against war and were for the defeat of the Russian government, rejected, however, such methods; these methods merely make it easier for the bourgeoisie to take repressive measure against Communists and revolutionary workers, and prevent the latter from winning over the toiling masses, especially the soldier masses, to the side of the mass struggle against imperialist war and for its transformation into civil war against the bourgeoisie.

The Seventh Congress of the Communist International, in outlining the tasks of the Communist Parties and of the entire working class in the event of war, bases itself upon the thesis advanced by Lenin and Rosa Luxemburg and adopted by the Stuttgart Congress of the pre-war Second International:

"If nevertheless war breaks out, it is their duty to work for its speedy termination and to strive with all their might to utilize the economic and political crisis produced by the war to rouse the masses of the people and thereby hasten the downfall of capitalist class rule."

At the present historical juncture, when on one-sixth part of the globe the Soviet Union defends Socialism and peace for all humanity, the most vital interests of the workers and toilers of all countries demand that in pursuing the policy of the working class, in waging the struggle for peace, the struggle against imperialist war before and after the outbreak of hostilities, the defense of the Soviet Union must be considered paramount.

If the commencement of a counter-revolutionary war forces the Soviet Union to set the Workers' and Peasants' Red Army in motion for the defense of Socialism, the Communists will call upon all toilers *to work, with all their means at their disposal and at any price, for the victory of the Red Army over the armies of the imperialists.*

Seventh World Congress of the Communist International, Resolutions on the Report of Ercoli, pp. 40-45.

www.ingramcontent.com/pod-product-compliance
Lightning Source LLC
Chambersburg PA
CBHW060203290526
45789CB00003B/1141